Surviving Years in Health and Social Care

of related interest

Risk and Risk Taking in Health and Social Welfare
Mike Titterton
ISBN 1 85302 482 1

Managing Sex Offender Risk
Edited by Hazel Kemshall and Gill McIvor
ISBN 1 84310 197 1
Research Highlights in Social Work 46

Working with Offenders
Edited by Gill McIvor
ISBN 1 85302 249 7
Research Highlights in Social Work 26

Managing Front Line Practice in Social Care
Edited by Daphne Statham
ISBN 1 85302 886 X
Research Highlights in Social Work 40

Stress in Social Work
Edited by Richard L. Davies
ISBN 1 85302 390 6

Staff Supervision in a Turbulent Environment
Managing Process and Task in Front-line Services
Lynette Hughes and Paul Pengelly
ISBN 1 85302 327 2

Good Practice in Adult Mental Health
Edited by Tony Ryan and Jacki Pritchard
ISBN 1 84310 217 X
Good Practice in Social Work 10

Good Practice in Working with Violence
Edited by Hazel Kemshall and Jacki Pritchard
ISBN 1 85302 641 7
Good Practice in Social Work 6

Surviving Fears in Health and Social Care

The Terrors of Night and the Arrows of Day

Martin Smith

Jessica Kingsley Publishers
London and Philadelphia

First published in the United Kingdom in 2005
by Jessica Kingsley Publishers
116 Pentonville Road
London N1 9JB, UK
and
400 Market Street, Suite 400
Philadelphia, PA 19106, USA
www.jkp.com

Copyright © Martin Smith 2005

Library of Congress Cataloging in Publication Data
Smith, Martin, 1958-
    Surviving fears in health and social care : the terrors of night and the arrows of day / Martin Smith.
        p. cm.
    Includes bibliographical references and index.
    ISBN 1-84310-180-7 (pbk.)
    1. Medical personnel—Mental health. 2. Medical personnel—Attitudes. 3. Medical person-nel—Psychology. 4. Social workers—Mental health. 5. Social workers—Attitudes. 6. Social workers—Psychology. 7. Fear. 8. Human services—Psychological aspects. I. Title.
    RC451.4.M44S64 2004
    610.69'6—dc22

                                                            2004022158

British Library Cataloguing in Publication Data
A CIP catalogue record for this book is available from the British Library

ISBN-13: 978 1 84310 180 2
ISBN-10: 1 84310 180 7

Printed and Bound in Great Britain by
Athenaeum Press, Gateshead, Tyne and Wear

To my parents

Acknowledgements

Linnet McMahon and Jean Nursten from The University of Reading helped inspire and nurture the belief that this book might be worthwhile and my confidence that I might be able to write it. Kay Clymo along with colleagues from *The British Journal of Social Work* and *The Journal of Social Work Practice* aided this process. In particular I would like to thank Andrew Cooper, Stephen Briggs and Lynn Froggett. Colleagues from Buckinghamshire Social Services have also been of help and encouragement: Eileen Springford, Patrick McGrath, Peter Cattanach and David Lees especially. Sheila, Robert, Jonathan and Verity were good company throughout the many phases of writing. Christina Anderson read a draft version of the book and made helpful comments.

I am indebted, most of all, to those who participated in the research studies described here and who shared their stories with me. Countless other service users, colleagues and students have helped me to become better acquainted with fear over the years. For these 'nameless acts of kindness', forgotten and remembered, many thanks.

Best safety lies in fear.

(Shakespeare, *Hamlet*)

Like one, that on a lonesome road
Doth walk in fear and dread,
And having once turned round walks on,
And turns no more his head;
Because he knows a frightful fiend
Doth close behind him tread.

(Samuel Taylor Coleridge, *The Rime of the Ancient Mariner*)

Ah yes, but that is not the real fear. The real fear is fear of what
lies beneath the surface of things, and this fear will not be dispelled.

(Franz Kafka, quoted in Beradt 1985)

Contents

Introduction

The Emerging Importance of Fear in Health and Social Care

This introduction begins with an identification of the book's intended readers. It continues with a recognition of how the author's life as a child and as a father has been shaped by his attempts to deal with fear. Ambivalent responses to fears are highlighted as is the need for available and responsive attachment figures to help us manage our fears. 'Fear' as a topic meriting investigation in its own right is seen to have emerged from research conducted into social workers' experiences of distress. The author's experiences as both social work practitioner and supervisor confirm this importance. A survey of relevant literature shows how fear has typically been considered as a part of another topic, leaving it ripe for consideration in its own right. A definition of fear follows and the introduction concludes with an overview of material to be found in future chapters.

Who is this book for and what will be gained from reading it?

This book is written with several different readers in mind. The need to be aware of fear and its potentially helpful and unhelpful manifestations can be likened to the need to be aware of the need for fire alarms in buildings to be tested and for occupants of such buildings to know what to do should the fire alarm sound. Although people frequently complain about fire drills they also recognize that the fire alarm is essentially there to promote their safety and, in extreme instances, even save their lives. Employees of an organization are usually told of fire alarm procedures and fire exits as part of their induction when beginning work. Established employees, irrespective of how many years they have worked for a company, need to participate regularly in fire drills when essential equipment is tested and escape strategies rehearsed. Employers have a duty to ensure that adequate procedures are in place and frequently tested. Employees have a duty to co-operate with such procedures so as to contribute responsibly to a safe work environment.

The analogy of the fire drill is an appropriate one for the understanding of differing 'levels' of health and social care workers who need to recognize fear and its manifestations. It is important that those on qualifying courses understand how fear is likely to affect them before they begin work as qualified professionals. They need to understand responses they might find themselves making and the importance of ensuring a safe exit should they be threatened by service users and find themselves unable to think, speak or move as a consequence of their fears. Such understanding should not be imparted in a 'scare tactic' manner but by way of provision of information that enables workers to be wise before, rather than after, the event and therefore better able to take steps to promote their safety. I have therefore been pleased to share some of the material in this book with students beginning and ending courses in health and social care and with employees new to an organization as part of their induction.

Awareness of the disabling capacity of fear merits recognition also by experienced workers. It does no harm for established workers to remind themselves that fear is no respecter of status as this can help them to guard against complacency and over-confidence. Several experienced social workers who believed they knew service users and enjoyed a good relationship with them have been tragically killed in recent years (Norris 1990), thinking that their 'good relationship' afforded them protection when it did not. Employers, managers and supervisors will also benefit from the enhanced understanding and appreciation of fear and ways in which it affects workers in health and social care, detailed in this book. Thinking of ways in which unwanted encounters with fear might be prevented and/or dealt with during and after events can aid staff recruitment and retention in organizations that are seen to be appropriately caring for their employees and thereby inspire trust and confidence. Employees to whom this understanding is communicated are likely to feel respected and valued, and want to remain with such organizations. Up until now, relatively little has been written that considers social care workers' experiences of fear 'head on' and this book makes a start in addressing that deficit. A particular issue that pervades the book is the need to distinguish the 'real' fear from the spurious, the helpful fear from the disabling and to consider when fear might be a useful friend to be encouraged rather than an enemy to be distanced. One difficulty in making this distinction is that workers might feel a genuine sense of real fear in relation to events imagined rather than encountered. Dealing sensitively with this issue is of crucial importance to the delivery of humane and effective staff care.

In addition to substantive quotations from research participants and relevant academic texts considerable use is made of literary and philosophical quotations throughout the book. These are included as they helpfully illuminate human beings' relationship with and responses to their fears. Fear is one of four 'basic emotions' (Ekman 2003) and, as such, is said to be recognizable across all cultures. Civilizations have been working with and contending against it for centuries and documenting these encounters in literary and philosophical writings which yield illuminating and potentially helpful insights into this relationship.

Fear and ambivalence

Fear is an emotion that most of us regard with ambivalence. We are drawn to it, fascinated with it and intrigued by it, while simultaneously being repelled by it, afraid of it and not wanting to know about it. Like the young child waking from a frightening dream we may not feel able to talk about our fears thinking them to be 'too scary'. We may worry that if we were to give words to that which disturbs us our attention may feed the fear and give it life, encouraging it to grow bigger and stronger so that it eventually threatens to overwhelm and incapacitate us. On the other hand, we may know the sheer weight-lifting relief that can accompany our sharing with and confiding in a trusted other, yearn for the comfort that this brings, and therefore feel compelled to talk about how we have been affected. Some people spend a lifetime ostensibly talking about their fears knowing that they are not getting close to the real dread that nestles, sleeping at the heart of their being like a slumbering dragon defying awakening.

Looking back, I can see several reasons why fear has been and is a topic of crucial importance for me. I recall, as a young child, waking repeatedly from nightmares featuring snakes and my father helping me deal with these by inventing funny names for the snakes that stalked my dreams and making jokes about them. When asked to complete a project at primary school I chose to investigate snakes and, along with another pupil who was researching lizards, went looking for them in my English county neighbourhood. Our searches were in vain and, unsurprisingly, we did not find any snakes (or lizards) in the small patch of waste land a few minutes distance from where we lived. I recall this memory here as I was to repeat this process in later life; in that being frightened of something I chose to look into it, find out about it and document and report my findings. Throughout the process of the school project I found my young mind increasingly fascinated by the rich variety of snakes that existed. I marvelled at their diversity and varying sizes, their colours and cultural differences; their adaptation to the climates they inhabited – water snakes, rattlesnakes, sea snakes, egg snakes, tree snakes, milk snakes... How some were small and fast and used deadly venom, how others were huge and crushed their prey to death, how some had distinctive markings and killed many people while others were relatively plain and harmless and just lay in the sun or moved through the grass.

Growing up, I dimly perceived a growing sense of the awe, dread and destruction that I later found portrayed in Shelley's [1818] (1986) 'Ozymandias of Egypt':

> ...Two vast and trunkless legs of stone
> Stand in the desert...
> And on the pedestal these words appear:
> 'My name is Ozymandias, king of kings:
> Look on my works, ye Mighty and despair!'
> Nothing beside remains. Round the decay
> Of that colossal wreck, boundless and bare,
> The lone and level sands stretch far away.

I can now see how some of these earlier memories influenced my more recent interest in the subject of fear. Now a father myself, I have tried to help my children talk about and understand their fears by attempting to think about their fears with them. Fears of young children are often particularly acute when related to the absence or unavailability of attachment figures.

Fears of children when attachment figures are not available

Bowlby (1973, p.200) writes, '...no fear-arousing situation is missed or camouflaged as often as fear that an attachment figure will be inaccessible or unresponsive.' Bowlby defines an attachment figure as someone who the child (or adult) regards as being bigger, stronger and better able to cope with the world than them. The individual therefore wants to attach (sometimes cling) to this person believing that this attachment will optimize their chances of survival.

Aged five, my daughter confirmed Bowlby's hypothesis. She was watching the film of *Jurassic Park* in which huge dinosaurs come to life and chase and kill terrified human beings. I was observing how relatively unafraid she seemed to be even at, what seemed to me to be, a particularly frightening part in the film when a huge Tyrannosaurus Rex was chasing one of the characters. In the dark and the rain the dinosaur towered over the hapless human with teeth white and gleaming. As if aware of what I was thinking she remarked, '*The Land Before Time* is much more scary than this.' I was surprised to hear her say this as although *The Land Before Time* is also about dinosaurs it is conveyed in cartoon animation which made it less frightening to me than the disturbingly realistic-looking scenes from *Jurassic Park*. When I asked my daughter why *The Land Before Time* was more scary she replied, 'Because there is an earthquake and Sarah [a young female dinosaur] can't get back to her mother.' This seems to support Bowlby's contention precisely.

On another occasion my son came home from school saying his sister had been crying when watching Disney's *Toy Story*. I talked with her about this and she said she had got upset at a point in the film where a cowboy toy asks for someone to 'lend him a hand' and a spaceman toy throws him his arm which had broken off. I recognized that there could be something upsetting about a broken arm or hand but knew she had seen this film several times previously at home on video and not become distressed by it then. I asked her why this was. She explained that while at home she had been near to one of her parents who were 'there for me'. When I suggested that there were teachers at school who were also 'there for her' in the classroom she replied that they were not only there for her, they were there for the other children as well so may have been busy elsewhere if and when she needed them. Again, Bowlby's claim about the importance of attachment figures can be seen to have relevance. With sufficiently close proximity to trusted attachment figures fear can be contained; without it, the same fear cannot be tolerated.

On another occasion my daughter and I were looking at a book on flower fairies together (Barker [1923] 1986). She was showing me her favourites, Buttercup, Foxglove, Wild Rose, Forget Me Not…when we came to the picture and words depicting Nightshade. She said, 'That's a horrible one – I'm going to tear it out of the book.' I found myself answering, 'No, don't do that. Although it's not very nice it's better that you know about it so that you can recognize it and not be hurt by it.' I later realized that these words encapsulated my motivation to research the nature and impact of fear in health and social care settings. It may be disturbing and frightening to open ourselves up to our fears in the hope of understanding them better. However, if we can get to know more about them and the ways in which they affect us we may be better able to deal with them and suffer their adverse and unwanted consequences less. This is a healthier response than to ignore them and pretend that they do not exist. The particular interest in researching fear in health and social care settings arose from a research study I conducted inquiring into social workers' experiences of distress (Smith and Nursten 1998).

Fear emerging from research into distress

Twenty-four qualified social workers from a variety of settings with an average of nine years post-qualified experience were asked by way of a semi-structured interview:

1. Describe an experience you have encountered throughout the course of your work that you have found distressing.

2. Describe the impact of this experience on you.

3. Describe what was helpful and unhelpful to you in attempting to deal with this experience.

4. Say what organizational systems and structures you think may help social workers affected by distressing experiences.

Of the 24 participants interviewed eight recalled a fear that they would be assaulted, four recalled a fear that someone else would be assaulted and three talked of having to respond to a request that made them feel afraid. Fear was the impact most commonly described in response to the second question. It became apparent that having been asked primarily about distress most people had talked most frequently about fear. I wondered why this should be. Could it be that fear and distress are closely related, even inter-twined, and that when people talk about distress they are actually, and also, talking about fear? It seemed that several social workers wanted to talk about their fears and had used, even welcomed, the opportunity to do so even if this was under the guise of something else – in this case distress. The findings from the research study into distress suggested the importance of fear so frequently and so powerfully that it seemed as if the subject of fear merited investigation in its own right. This view was borne out by reflecting upon my own experiences of working in health and social care settings.

Fear emerging from experiences as a social work practitioner

Reviewing my social work career I recognized how profoundly experiences of fear, in particular, could vividly engage with and remain in the mind. When beginning work with service users suffering from schizophrenia I saw a young man in his early twenties who told me that he had seen God and the Devil in his bedroom the previous night and that they had been talking to him. Thinking that it would be helpful to explore what lay behind this communication I asked what they looked like. 'The Devil looked like a satyr and God looked like a wise old man,' he told me. I asked what they said to him and he replied that the Devil attempted to tempt him into doing bad things against God. At this point I wondered if he might present a danger to himself and/or others as a result of what he had been hearing. I therefore asked him what, exactly, the Devil had said. His demeanour and appearance suddenly changed in response to this question. He abruptly sat up straight and looked worried and edgy. He said he couldn't possibly tell me what the Devil had said. Why, I wondered, given how willing to talk and forthcoming he had been previously. 'Because, if I tell you that they'll appear here now,' he answered, 'oh, no…' he continued, staring wide-eyed and hard just beyond my shoulder, '…they're here, behind you'. I felt a shiver run up (or down?) my spine and found myself turning around to look in the direction of his gaze. Even at the time I was aware of asking myself why I was turning around to look and trying to convince myself that I didn't *really* expect to see God and the Devil in the room (did I?). I do not recall how the interview was ended but the incident has remained in my mind as a powerful reminder of how potent experiences of fear can be, whatever the thought *reality* and how they can make us act in ways which take us by surprise.

I can also remember being extremely frightened when interviewing a young man in his early twenties for the purposes of a mental health act assessment. He had arrived at his mother's house unexpectedly and was talking in a bizarre and deluded manner. He had caused considerable damage to her property and the police had been called. When I arrived there was a policeman sat either side of him on a sofa. The young man was stirring restlessly on the sofa between the policemen and was chewing on a biro slowly and deliberately. He did not look at me or answer my questions but just kept chewing slowly, occasionally shooting me a glance from underneath hooded eyelids. Over many years of experience of interviewing people with a wide variety of mental disorders in community settings I had rarely been so well protected nor felt so acutely afraid. I imagined the young man suddenly springing like a large cat across the room to get me, stabbing me in the throat with the biro, while the policemen, open-mouthed and too slow to react, could do nothing but sit by helplessly and watch.

The young man began to talk, slowly and deliberately, expressing pain and unhappiness about a failed relationship with a woman who was the mother of his young daughter. He claimed she was preventing him from seeing his daughter and talked in a disjointed fashion about visiting a grave but it was hard to make sense of what he was trying to communicate. His mother, standing in the room next to him, looked down on him sorrowfully, unable to help explain or elaborate. Abruptly the young man's conversation changed, he talked urgently and with fervour, claiming that strangers were entering his flat at night without his permission. He went on to say, 'Someone has been coming into my bed at night and raping me...and that person is you.' He looked directly at me and again, I felt a cold shiver. I found myself thinking, 'There's no way out of this – I'm done for, he's not going to listen to any argument from me protesting my innocence. In any event, how could I defend myself against an accusation like that?'

I cannot recall what was probably a fumbled response but the interview continued and he did not jump across the room to get me. He was subsequently admitted to an acute psychiatric ward without incident. While there was a sense in which 'nothing had happened' in the 'real', external world a great deal had taken place inside my head. Another finding from the research into distress was that participants described their 'imagination running riot' as one of the most troubling impacts of distressing experiences and I had certainly encountered that here. I understood then how profoundly disappointing and deflating it can be to return from an incident like this to be told by a preoccupied supervisor or manager, 'Well, nothing *actually* happened, did it?' While it may be true in one respect that 'nothing happened' in another way a great deal has happened and human beings are often more affected by what they imagine could have transpired than by what actually did. This is particularly relevant to a consideration of fear which is future-based. Unlike guilt and regret which look to the past and to what has or has not happened fear looks ahead to what might happen or what might have happened and is therefore future-orientated.

More recently I was asked to see Nina (a pseudonym), who was in her late thirties and had worked as a residential social worker in a children's home. She had been assaulted at work by two young women and had been diagnosed as suffering from Post Traumatic Stress Disorder. She was told by her doctor that she would never be able to return to residential social work. Nina wrote a 22-page letter to the Director of Social Services explaining how she felt and telling of how she and her family had been affected by what had happened. She was asking for some recognition of how she felt and some help to try to deal with it. She particularly identified the prevailing predominance of fear as the following extract from her letter (quoted with her permission) illustrates:

> All through this experience I have come across feelings and fears that I did not realize I could have. It is not easy to admit to yourself or others that you are unable to travel far from home without the support from your husband for fear of getting into a panic. It is hard to get used to the idea that you are unable to go out in public places because of fear, fear that it is hard to explain at times, even to yourself. I find it hard that after all these months I am still unable to do the things I have done for years.

I worked with Nina over 20 months, initially visiting her in her home as she felt too frightened to leave it. One of the effects of the assault was to make her feel that the outside world had become an unsafe place which could no longer be trusted. She felt her house had been turned into a prison, patrolled by invisible jailors. She repeatedly and obsessively decorated the inside of this prison, rubbing down surfaces and painting her rooms with dark and gloomy shades that she later told me she did not like but which spoke for her mood. She would awake in the early hours of the morning, convinced that the young people who had assaulted her were downstairs. She rushed downstairs to confront them, finding no one there.

I sensed a great ambivalence from her towards me. She welcomed my visits in that I was employed by and represented the department she had once worked for and thus kept alive the link she wanted to preserve between her and the department. On the other hand, I was able still to work for the department while she was not. I was therefore envied, resented, even hated, because of this. Nina also told me later that after I, or any one else from the 'outside world', had visited her she would hurriedly vacuum the floor once we had left as if we had brought in with us something contaminating, corrupting, that she wanted rid of: something unbearable that she could not tolerate.

After my visiting Nina on several occasions we agreed that it was not helpful for us to continue to meet in her house. To do so seemed to confirm her in the prison she wanted to be free from. Nina set herself two objectives for our work; she wanted to trace her steps back to the unit where she used to work and she wanted to visit the busy city centre shopping area near where she lived without experiencing a panic attack. We therefore began to walk to her previous place of work together, going just as far as she felt able to manage on the day, turning back when she felt she had 'had enough' yet getting a little nearer each time.

On one occasion we encountered several adolescent children pushing and pulling one another in a playful but boisterous way. Suddenly I was aware of becoming hyper-vigilant, I sensed threat and feared danger, I became wary and looked for an exit. We walked past the young people without incident but the ways in which they affected me gave me a clue as to how Nina probably felt in relation to them and the memories they evoked. I do not think I would have felt this way were I there on my own and this experience provided an example of how powerfully those experiencing fear can project these feelings into others nearby (try sitting next to someone who is afraid of flying on an aeroplane for any length of time and not feeling affected by their fear!).

On another occasion Nina and I walked past a large, disused hotel. She told me, 'I know it sounds stupid but the kids used to play in there and when I walked past it I expected a large hand to come out of it, grab me and pull me inside.' In articulating this fear Nina was drawing on an archetype (Fordham 1966) of fear which has been much employed by horror novels and films; supernatural hands reaching through walls to attack humans on the other side. She 'knew' (rationally) that this was not going to happen yet it did not prevent her from fearing it. All we consciously 'know' about our fears does not protect us from their influence. Many people know that they are less likely to come to harm when flying rather than driving but this does not prevent them from feeling safer when driving rather than flying.

We eventually walked sufficiently close to the unit where Nina used to work for her to be able to see it which she said was enough for her. She did not want to actually enter the unit again. As our meetings continued she gained sufficient confidence to visit the shopping centre near where she lived. We went for coffee in a busy department store and a woman from another table asked Nina to pass the sugar which she did. Once out of the store Nina could barely conceal her delight: 'Did you see that? That woman asked me to pass the sugar and I did! She didn't even know there was anything wrong with me! She thought I was *normal*.' This reaction helped me to see how deeply the shame and embarrassment that frequently attend fear-provoking experiences can run. I imagined that Nina must have walked around thinking she bore a public proclamation of the experience she had suffered, something that everyone would see and recognize and therefore know immediately what had happened to her; a modern-day scarlet letter (Hawthorne [1850] 1986). Feeling free from this awful stigma was an important step for her to take in recognizing that she did not need to be in thrall to her fear for ever.

My experiences of working with Nina, including her initial identification of fear as being crucial to her state of mind along with the many facets and repercussions of fear which she showed me throughout our time together, confirmed my notion that fear is an essential aspect of work in health and social settings meriting investigation.

In addition to experiences when working as a social work practitioner confirming my view that fear merited its own consideration I also recalled a number of instances when working as a supervisor of social workers which confirmed this hypothesis.

Fear emerging from experiences as a supervisor of social workers

A male supervisee was telling me of an occasion when he was interviewing a service user diagnosed as suffering from schizophrenia. The service user was normally forthcoming in response to being interviewed but had inexplicably gone quiet. Looking directly at the social worker he suddenly said that he knew the social worker had been sent by the Devil to put bad thoughts into his head. The worker's response was similar to my own, recounted above, when I was told that God and the Devil had appeared in the room. How could he begin to defend himself against such an accusation? He could not possibly *prove* it untrue. He acknowledged how it could have been much worse. At least the service user had decided to tell him what he thought; he could have entertained the thoughts without giving words to them and attacked him instead. Again fear can be seen as a perception about what could have happened as much as, if not more than, what actually did happen.

A different kind of fear was expressed by a female social worker working in a mental health team whom I was supervising when we were discussing whether or not she could work with a service user who had been sexually abused. She was reluctant to undertake this work and while we were exploring this told me that this was because she had been sexually abused by an uncle when younger. She asked me not to share this information with my (female) line manager. I initially agreed with her request not to share what she had told me appreciating that she would want as few people as possible to know about her past abuse. However, as time went on I felt increasingly uncomfortable about this. She and I both knew my manager to be a reasonable and fair person and one who could be trusted to respond to such information with tact, discretion and sensitivity. I felt I was being treated as a potentially abusing male who was perpetuating a guilty secret. This seemed to mirror the 'secret' her uncle had told her to keep.

I discussed the dilemma with a female colleague and as a result of this told the supervisee that my manager needed to know what she had told me. However, I also said that I was open as to how the manager was informed and requested that the worker told her directly herself, with or without me present. The supervisee's reaction was an extreme one. She said, 'That's it then! If you tell her I'll be finished as a social worker! Who will employ me then? You may as well publish it in the staff newsletter. I may as well dance naked on the table. Is that what you want?' I was not prepared for a reaction of such force and magnitude. It seemed that I had activated a deep and profound fear that was out of context and proportion to what we were discussing. We eventually agreed that the two of us would see the manager together and that the supervisee would explain the matter.

The manager was understanding and supportive and my relationship with the supervisee subsequently emerged from the darkness of hidden secrecy into a more positively open, mutually satisfactory experience. The levels and overlapping, multi-faceted nature of fears are apparent here. First, there was her fear of working with the service user that concealed a deeper and more fundamental fear of her previous sexual abuse coming to light. When she had told of the abuse there was the fear of repercussions, projected, inappropriately and unreasonably, into myself and my manager. My fear was of being seen as an abusing male who was carrying an unhealthy secret but also of being seen as an abusing male were I to share the secret. Once again, an enhanced understanding of the nature, manifestations and workings of fear seemed as if it might be helpful. By giving fear appropriate words at appropriate times, in appropriate contexts, we had all moved on to benefit.

Prompted by the thought that fear may be a comparatively under-researched, under-written about topic despite its profundity and prevalence in health and social care I turned to the literature to see whether this was, in fact, the case.

Fear in relevant literature

Although fear does feature in the health and social care literature it is more likely to do so as a sub-heading in the context of another topic that is under consideration. Examples are when working with people with mental illness (Binder 1991; Levey and Howells 1995; Prins 1988) or in child protection work (Department of Health 1991; Frosh 1987; London Borough of Brent 1985) or when working in potentially dangerous situations (Balloch, Pahl and McLean 1998; Bibby 1994). Scott and Stradling (1993) have written of fears that may feature when counselling those suffering Post Traumatic Stress Disorder and Sinason (1994) of the extreme form that fears can take when working with those alleging Satanist abuse. In the counselling literature fears are also described but again, in relation to something else, such as debt counselling (Mann 1992), work in a youth club (Chapman 1992), death and the mid-life crisis (Magilner 1996) and intercultural therapy and counselling (Gordon 1996). Buyssen (1996) claims that, although nurses routinely encounter traumatic experiences that make them feel afraid, accounts of these experiences had not previously been collected and analysed. Given its prevalence fear seems to be under-represented in the literature and when it is written of it is usually done so indirectly.

An exception to this general trend not to consider fear directly can be seen in the *No fear* campaign launched by *Community Care* magazine in 1999. This campaign was based on the premises that workers in health and social care had a right to work safely, without being threatened and intimidated by service users and that an unfortunate tendency for some to see threats and violence as forming 'part of the job' needed to be challenged. Braithwaite (2001, p.60), a frequent contributor to the campaign, claims, 'All staff have a right to perform their job free from violence or the fear of violence.' *Community Care* was 'declaring war on violence' (Smith 2002). It was unusual to see the word 'fear' frequently appear on the front of a magazine with a wide circulation among those working in health and social care settings and this was, arguably, a good thing as it highlighted the importance of considering fear in its own right. However, while drawing attention to fear the campaign was simultaneously dismissing it, contending that it was not wanted and that workers would be better off without it, being able to work with *no fear*.

This book differs from the *Community Care* campaign by arguing that, although at times distressing and disabling, fear has many aspects and some of them are life-enhancing and even life-saving. Those who truly live with no fear are soon seriously injured or dead. To live without fear is not helpful. To live with an enhanced understanding of it and how it affects us, is. This book will aid the reader to get better acquainted with fear in the belief that the more we can understand it and get to know it the better we can work with it and it can work for us. We need to begin with a definition.

To define true fear...

'Fear' is an extremely complex word to define. LeDoux (1998, p.129) writes:

> Even a casual analysis of the number of ways the concept of fear can be expressed in the English language reveals its importance in our lives: alarm, scare, worry, concern, misgiving, qualm, disquiet, uneasiness, wariness, nervousness, edginess, jitteriness, apprehension, anxiety, trepidation, fright, dread, anguish, panic, terror, horror, consternation, distress, unnerved, distraught, threatened, defensive.

Of these 27 near neighbours of fear 'anxiety' is particularly likely to be used in place of 'fear'. Sometimes the words seem to be used interchangeably such as in the title of Marks' (1980) *Living with Fear: Understanding and Coping with Anxiety*. In the index of Klein's *The Psycho-Analysis of Children* [1932] (1975, pp.305,296) under 'fear' can be found, 'see anxiety, see also phobia(s)' while under 'anxiety' reads, 'anxiety/fear'.

There does, however, seem to be some agreement that fear is more likely to be experienced in relation to a recognizable and specific danger or threat while anxiety is a state of tension generated without the existence of such recognizable external triggers. Freud (1959, p.165) encapsulates this thought: 'Anxiety (Angst)...has a quality of indefiniteness and lack of object. In precise speech we use the word fear (Furcht) rather than anxiety if it has found an object.' However, even this distinction entails difficulties as indicated by an editor's note (Freud 1959, p.165):

> It has not been possible in translation to render the German 'Angst' invariably by 'anxiety'. In this volume...the word has sometimes been translated by 'fear' or by phrases including the word 'afraid' where English usage required it and confusion seemed unlikely.

These difficulties are further compounded by the fact that the states of anxiety and fear may occur together, making telling them apart even more difficult (Erikson [1951] 1977).

Despite the elusiveness of a precise definition, the basic distinction between fear as being a response to something recognizable, specific and external and anxiety as being less obviously determined and internal remains. Phillips (1997, p.59), a contemporary psychodynamic writer claims, 'One of the aims of psychoanalysis is to turn anxiety back into fear... Fear has an object, anxiety has a vague location. Anxiety is a defence against fear, a refusal to know what we are frightened of.'

Doctor and Kahn (1989, p.185) offer a comprehensive definition of fear:

> Fear is an emotion of uneasiness that arises as a normal response to a perceived threat that may be real or imagined. Fear involves an outer behavioural expression, an inner feeling and physiological changes. The word *fear* comes from the Old English word *faer* meaning sudden calamity or danger and refers to justified fright. Fear may cause a variety of unpleasant feelings including terror, a desire to escape, a pounding heart, muscular tenseness, trembling, dryness of the throat and mouth, a sinking feeling in the stomach, nausea, perspiration, difficulty in breathing, feelings of unreality, paralysing weakness of the limbs, a sensation of faintness and falling, a sudden urge to urinate or defecate or a great urge to cry. Fear may induce certain types of behaviour, such as flight, fighting or concealment. Chronic fear in healthy people may result in fatigue, depression, slowing down of mental processes, restlessness, aggression, loss of appetite, insomnia and nightmares. Fear is a normal and useful emotion. When one faces a threat fear often leads to rapid action, such as fighting back or removing oneself from the scene. Fear can also motivate learning and performance of socially useful responses such as careful driving or completing an examination.

The detail and length of this definition is both its attraction and its difficulty. Inspired by the thought that fear is a fascinating and complex concept open to various and multi-faceted interpretation I set out to attempt to discover what those working in health and social care meant when they talked of fear. Using a semi-structured interview devised for the purpose I asked 72 participants working in health and social care settings:

1.   Talk about a time, or times, when you experienced fear in your work.

2.   How did this experience affect you?

3.   How did you respond to it?

4.   What helped you to deal with the experience, generally, and what was unhelpful?

5.   What are the responses you would like from an *ideal supervisor* with whom you discussed a fear-provoking experience?

6.   If you were looking at a picture entitled 'Fear in social work/counselling' what would you see?

Responses from participants did not disappoint and will be referred to frequently throughout the following chapters of this book, the contents of which are as follows.

Overview of the chapters that follow

Each of the following chapters begins with a summary introduction and ends with recommendations for practice and training. 'He' and 'she' have been used in alternate chapters to avoid the cumbersome 'he or she'.

Chapter One, 'Reasons to be Fearful', establishes a vantage point from which later chapters can be viewed by considering the filters of early childhood experience and culture through which health and social care workers inevitably see their fears. Ways in which fears are communicated to babies and young infants by way of nursery rhymes and fairy tales are considered as is the pervading influence of some nineteenth-century British horror novels. The fact that people sometimes seek out, welcome and pay for fear is acknowledged. The importance of the visual image as a signifier of the fear experience is highlighted but so too is the possibility that workers will be more frightened by what they do not see than by what they do – such is the 'shaping spirit' of the imagination. The influences of Jung's collective unconscious and the shadow (Fordham 1966) on people's fears are illustrated.

Chapter Two considers fear in relation to child care and child protection work in community settings. The influence of ambivalence in relation to fear is traced again through reports of inquiries into child deaths. On the one hand ways in which fear can cloud professional judgement are acknowledged; on the other hand professionals are exhorted to continue to function rationally and effectively despite the corrosive impact of fear and its repercussions. An important thread running throughout the book is how the imagination 'running riot' can bring threats to life and this phenomenon is introduced in this chapter. In extreme cases this 'running riot' is shown to be fatal. Fears of physical assault and of workers losing control are also illustrated in this chapter.

Fears particularly relating to mental health work are illustrated in Chapter Three. In addition to fundamental fears of separation from helpful attachment figures outside, fears of annihilation from inside the individual are highlighted. Fear inspired as a result of the imagination running riot is illustrated again as are fears of death, experienced by workers in extreme circumstances.

Chapter Four discusses fears that arise from working with vulnerable adults in community settings. Fears of experiencing violence at the hands of service users are illustrated as is the dis-inhibiting influence of alcohol and substance abuse. Threats posed by older people are given particular consideration in this chapter.

Fears arising from work undertaken in residential and institutional settings are the focus of Chapter Five. Fears of death are again apparent as is the influence of the 'gothic' (Botting 1996) on the way in which people recall their fears. Fears of sexual assault and the attendant shame and embarrassment that accompany these are illustrated as is the sometimes 'primitive' desire for retaliation and revenge that can be evoked in response to feeling that one is under threat in extreme circumstances.

Chapter Six considers fear in the organizational context where fears of complaints and, particularly, complaints procedures are shown to be potent and disabling. Sometimes buildings, rather than people, come under attack from service users giving rise to understandable fears for those inside and examples of this are given in this chapter. Fears arising from perceived bullying in the workplace are also considered.

Chapter Seven is the first of two chapters looking at what workers found to be helpful when attempting to deal with their fears. Support from one's colleagues and peer group are considered to be the single most helpful response to fear and reasons for this are given in this chapter and examples provided. Supervision is considered in some detail because of its intended pivotal role in health and social care. Fear-provoking experiences affect workers' families as well as the workers themselves and the parts played by family members are also considered in this chapter.

The second chapter considering what workers found helpful in the aftermath of fear-provoking experiences, Chapter Eight highlights the importance of management within a workplace culture. Workers experiencing fear are likely to experience a child-like response to their fears and therefore turn for help to those perceived to be in parental roles. Past experiences can be brought into workers' expectations of how they should be treated and managers and their workers need to be aware of these processes at work. The importance of police involvement, both during and after incidents, reflection, humour and the research process itself is also considered in this chapter. The chapter ends by identifying possible useful further areas of research into fear while respecting the fact that some people prefer to deal with their fears by not talking about them.

The Afterword argues that although fear might be a tyrannical master it can also be a wonderful servant. As well as being something unpleasant to be avoided fear can also be a helpful, life-preserving gift. It is a question of degree. Rather than thinking of fear as either a good or a bad thing, it depends on the circumstances and the time. The crucial thing for workers in health and social care is to get to know fear more intimately and strive for the discernment necessary to fear the right thing to the right extent, at the right time, in the right way.

Chapter 1

Reasons to be Fearful

Introduction

This chapter begins by tracing origins of fundamental fears back to early life when these are communicated to babies and young infants by way of lullabies, nursery rhymes and fairy tales. British horror novels of the nineteenth century are then considered as this genre has proved particularly influential in formulating archetypes of fear which have been constantly reproduced and re-interpreted since their original creations. Prevailing themes of the over-reacher, the discoverer and pursuit in horror plots are observed and links made with work in health and social care. Recognition of ways in which fears are portrayed in contemporary film then follows. The depiction of different types of fears by famous artists – Bosch, Goya, Blake, Munch and Harvey – is briefly discussed. The chapter ends by highlighting two crucial contributions from C.G. Jung to an understanding of fear – that of the collective unconscious and the shadow.

Cultural filters through which we see and understand our fears

Health and social care workers, along with all other human beings, will inevitably experience and envisage fears through culturally determined filters and contexts. We are taught to be afraid by means of archetypal signifiers which symbolize and embody the nature and impact of the fear experience. Many of the images of fear are stored in our minds and memories in a visual form representing something we have seen or imagined. The cinematic attention to detail with which many memories of fear-provoking experiences are recounted by participants later in the book bears testament to the crucial importance of the visual image as a means of picturing and conveying memory.

Literature, art and film have produced and reproduced many of these images.

Literature

Warner (2000) shows how the infant's need to be afraid is communicated by the destructive and sometimes murderous sentiments to be found in nursery rhymes. Paradoxically these are expressed in the gentle singing of a lullaby by a loving parent or carer, providing another example of the ambivalence which permeates an understanding of fear:

> Rock a-bye baby on the tree top,
> When the wind blows the cradle will rock;
> When the bough breaks the cradle will fall,
> Down will come cradle and baby and all.

These words communicate the perilous nature of the baby's existence and the need, therefore, to be fearful but do so by way of a soothing tune sung as a soft, affectionate, reverie. Sometimes words of nursery rhymes warn of danger from predatory enemies rather than from 'accidental' falling should the baby be too noisy or not sufficiently good:

> Baby, baby, naughty baby,
> Hush you squalling thing, I say.
> Peace this moment, peace, or maybe
> Bonaparte will pass this way.

> Baby, baby, he's a giant,
> Tall and black as Rouen steeple,
> And he breakfasts, dines, rely on't,
> Every day on naughty people.

> And he'll beat you, beat you, beat you,
> And he'll beat you all to pap,
> And he'll eat you, eat you, eat you,
> Every morsel, snap, snap, snap.

Warner suggests that the combination of the fear-provoking words and the soothing tune that accompanies these enables those caring for the young infant to communicate their anger and rage to the child in a context of love and tenderness:

> In such a song, the singer's violent and violating narrative is at variance with the music and the lullaby's prime function, for if the baby could understand the words, she or he would be likely to wake up with a start of terror, far from lulled. But if the child is still an infant, the words are likely not to be understood: as the mother or grandmother or nurse or sibling sings rockingly, caressingly, she is able to give vent to her anger, and often her exhaustion at the task – without the child taking in the words. (Warner 2000, p.220)

Bettelheim (1979) and Tatar (2003) show how fairy tales initiate young children into a world of fear as they depict protagonists being exposed to, and usually triumphing over, their worst fears; Hansel and Gretel contending with parental abandonment in the woods, Red Riding Hood face to face with the predatory wolf, Snow White being threatened by her murderous step-mother, Beauty transforming the beast, Cinderella suffering at the hands of her step-sisters, Jack and his mother facing poverty and destitution all show the infant or young(er) child facing fearful and possible fatal possibilities and surviving them by virtue of their wits, goodness or the (often unexpected and unusual) help of others. Bettelheim (1979) argues that these fairy tales will always retain their popularity with children because they recognize, despite their young years, that crucially important life struggles and difficulties are depicted in and by them.

While fears have been written of in many various shapes and forms throughout the years nineteenth-century British horror novels are a particularly fertile genre for the generation of archetypes which have been constantly reworked and re-interpreted ever since. Carroll writes that horror stories are:

> ...predominantly concerned with knowledge as a theme. The two most frequent families of plot structures are those of the complex discovery cluster and the over-reacher cluster... A great deal of the sustaining interest in horror stories concerns the discovery of the unknown. The majority of horror stories are, to a significant extent, representations of processes of discovery. (Carroll 1990, p.127)

While this description holds true for horror stories the roles of discoverer and over-reacher have relevance also to work in health and social care where people are also concerned with 'the discovery of the unknown'. Much interviewing, assessment and counselling is intended to discover (search out), or enlarge understanding of service users, their families and circumstances as workers attempt to uncover previously unknown or unacknowledged material to benefit without over-reaching in the process. Looking back on my own experience when interviewing the service user who claimed to have seen God and the Devil appear to him in his room the previous evening (see Introduction), I can see that my fear was at least partly that I had over-reached in my attempts to discover. I was afraid of the terrible consequences I might have unwittingly unleashed as a consequence of my well-intentioned but foolish blundering.

The over-reacher plot in horror stories shows an individual (often a doctor or scientist) who wants to explore beyond the previously established limits of what is known or possible. The over-reacher then creates a character which successfully breaks new ground but with such awful consequences that its creator regrets what he has done and is eventually killed by his creation. Shelley's [1818] (1994) *Frankenstein* and Stevenson's [1886] (1974) *The Strange Case of Dr Jekyll and Mr Hyde* are examples of the over-reacher. Dr Frankenstein articulates the motivation which led to him creating the monster:

> The world was to me a secret which I desired to divine. Curiosity, earnest research to learn the hidden laws of nature…as they were unfolded to me, are among the earliest sensations I can remember… I have always been embued with a fervent longing to penetrate the secrets of nature… (Shelley [1818] 1994, pp.22–28)

This 'longing to penetrate the secrets of nature' also inspired Dr Jekyll's experiments which culminated in the creation/discovery of Mr Hyde, his shadow self. The central discovery by Dr Jekyll that 'Man is not truly one but truly two' (Stevenson [1886] 1974, p.102) encapsulates the origins of much inquiry that has been conducted since into the multiplicity of human nature (Sinason 2002). For Dr Jekyll however, as for Dr Frankenstein, the discoveries that he could give life to a new creation resulted in his death as he over-reached what was his to know. As Carroll (1990, p.118) remarks:

> The over-reacher plot is concerned with forbidden knowledge of either the scientific or the magical sort...the recurring theme of the over-reacher plot is that there is some knowledge better left to the gods (or whomever).

In this sense the over-reacher plot recalls the injunction given by God to Adam in the garden of Eden, '...of the tree of the knowledge of good and evil you are not to eat, for on the day you eat of it you shall most surely die' (Genesis 2:17).

The Hound of the Baskervilles (Conan Doyle [1902] 1996) and *Dracula* (Stoker [1897] 1996) provide examples of the discoverer plot. In these novels Holmes and Watson and Harker and Van Helsing learn that the hound and the vampire are up to no good and set out to discover more so that they can put an end to their evil influences. While both over-reacher and discoverer plots entail pursuit this is particularly evident in the discoverer plot. The hound and vampire pursue their quarry while they are pursued in turn by their would-be discoverers. Holmes and Watson leave London for Dartmoor in pursuit of the hound and Count Dracula is pursued from Transylvania to Whitby to London and back to Transylvania again. Health and social care workers are often pursuing their service users/patients either literally or metaphorically (and sometimes both!). They are attempting to bring to light new knowledge and awareness that will lead to enhanced understanding, more appropriate responses and relationships more conducive to good work. These novels act as a salutary reminder that while discovery is all well and good the potential danger of over-reaching needs to be constantly borne in mind.

Much horror writing constitutes part of the gothic tradition (Punter 1996). Botting (1996, p.9) claims that the gothic genre appeals because it combines representations of the truly frightening with a subtle blend of ridicule and desire:

> Its images of dark power and mystery evoked fear and anxiety, but their absurdity also provoked ridicule and laughter. The emotions most associated with Gothic fiction are similarly ambivalent: objects of terror and horror not only provoke repugnance, disgust and recoil, but also engage readers' interest, fascinating and attracting them. Threats are spiced with thrills, terrors with delights, horrors with pleasures.

This quotation acknowledges that interest, fascination and attraction might be as much a part of the fear experience as threats, terrors and horrors. Indeed, that fear might actually be sought out for a number a reasons, perhaps to add 'spice to life', perhaps as means of attempting to get re-acquainted with or to work through childhood fears. The horror novel and film industry are financially lucrative businesses which flourish because readers and viewers are prepared to pay money in order to be frightened. Another reason why we are fearful is that, at times, we want to be, and will therefore seek out frightening experiences if we feel sufficient lack of them in our lives. Going to see a horror film is one example of this vicarious engagement.

Film

Rigby (2000) claims that the horror film is Britain's shaping cinematic myth, as the western is America's. In *Hearths of Darkness* Williams (1996) argues that, in more recent years, the true source of genuine fear in films is located, not outside human beings by way of a monster or vampire, but inside them, in their conceptions of themselves and their relationships with one another.

Ward (1996, p.273) writes, 'It is a strange sociological fact that there are people who are paid especially to devise ways to scare us out of our wits.' These people would not be paid unless there were people willing to finance them. The fact that people will pay at the cinema box office or video rental shop with the specific intent of being frightened and the accompanying desire for this keeps the horror film makers in business. Ward (1996, p.271) acknowledges this willing and active participation of the viewer of horror films:

> ...the viewer of a work of art is not a passive receptacle but an active par-
> ticipant, mobilising all the forces of the unconscious mind in actively
> apprehending the work. The films tap into unconscious reservoirs of
> feeling on the one hand and broad mythological themes on the other.

Walsh (2003, p.56), writing of the profound influence that films can have on the individual's development, explores why people would want to be frightened by horror films: 'We dare ourselves not to be scared by the demons lurking on screen. We test, in some perverse way, our capacity to become, voluntarily, gibbering wrecks when confronted by our own paranoia.' Horror films afford an opportunity to expose ourselves to our fears, alone or in the company of chosen others, for a limited time in relative safety. With the disturbance of exposure comes the possibility of mastery. Horror films can therefore help people to manage and even transcend their fears. The risk one runs is that of unwittingly embedding recurring images in the memory which cannot be shaken off and which, 'move slowly through our minds by day and are the trouble of our dreams' (Wordsworth [1805] 1970, Book 1, line 427).

The recurrent situations repeatedly re-invented in horror films such as fears of being alone, isolation, darkness, madness, the 'alien', the satanic, possession, ghosts from the past and intimations of the future encapsulate and communicate the essential elements of our fears. Very often, the fear experience is heightened by *not showing* the source of the fear. Dimly lit corridors, empty doorways, vacant stairways are often portrayed to the accompaniment of suitably disturbing music. The reason for this is that the film makers know that we are likely to be more effectively frightened by what we supply to fill the spaces from our imaginations than we will be by anything they can provide. Often the eventual revelation of the monster or bogey comes as something of an anti-climax. This is relevant to an understanding of fears experienced by workers in health and social care. Such is the power of the imagination that what they *do not see* and what *does not happen* might actually be more frightening than 'the reality'.

Imagination is also supplied by visual images which feature in works of art, recognized to be of importance and validity by people looking at them.

Art

Films and pictures are such powerful mediums for conveying fears because human beings are fundamentally influenced by images; arguably, they are more profoundly influenced by images than words. Berger (1972, p.7) traces the pervading influence of the visual back to early life: 'Seeing comes before words. The child looks and recognises before it can speak.' Daley (1984, p.xiii) claims that people can not only see images, they can also project them in a visual form:

> Man's most fundamental thoughts and feelings, derived from the unconscious, reach expression in images rather than words...every individual,

whether trained or untrained in art, has a latent capacity to project his inner conflicts into visual forms.

'The mind's eye' sees deep and shows us our worst fears as images. Many famous artists have projected different aspects of fear into visual forms which have since been incorporated into and assimilated by culture and tradition. Hieronymous Bosch (1450–1516) painted half-human, half-animal forms engaging in torture, murder, cannibalism and depravity. One of his intentions in painting in this way was to frighten the viewer of the picture into avoiding the excesses of sin. In a time and place when most people could not read or write, Bosch's visual sermons conveyed a fearful and powerful message.

Towards the end of his life Francisco Goya (1746–1828) created memorable scenes of fantasy and terror. His paintings convey the horrors of war and of social and cultural breakdown as deranged, destructive evil runs amok in human, mythological and Satanic guises. 'The Sleep of Reason Brings Forth Monsters' depicts nightmarish forms arising from the sleeping figure showing that under the thin veil of reason and order fear of the monstrous lurks, just waiting to surface and take control.

William Blake (1757–1827) attempted to show fears of human frailty and disintegration in the context of awe and holy dread. 'The Ancient of Days' shows a formidable creating force demanding worship and obedience. 'God Judging Adam' represents the expulsion from a symbolic rather than a literal Eden along with anticipated fears of being separated from the beneficence of an all-powerful creator father. 'Nebuchadnezzar' shows an abandoned derangement in the wide staring eyes of the previously respected but now destitute king embodying fears of a fall from grace and consequent madness. Blake's pictures of the 'tyger' are not particularly frightening but in the poem of the same name he reflects upon the tyger as a representation of creative energy that is to be reverenced along with its destructive aspects that are to be feared in awe.

Munch's (1863–1944) *The Scream* conveys one of the most memorable visual depictions of the fear of mental disintegration and inner annihilation. In *Angst* he shows featureless and barely human dark, gathering figures who seem to bode some brooding evil. The fear shown in this picture is that of groups, crowds, perhaps of the unfathomable bureaucracies written of by Kafka [1925] (1978).

More recently the artist Marcus Harvey exhibited a depiction of the child killer Myra Hindley made up of children's hand prints at the Royal Academy of Arts in London in 1997. The family of one of Hindley's victims requested that the work was not exhibited. The request was refused and the picture vandalized twice within a week. The debate about what fears can reasonably be portrayed for public consumption in artistic forms is a complex and multi-faceted one. The artist might claim he is merely bringing to attention the fears that lie beneath awareness, the viewer might respond that some things should not be shown in the interests of good taste and decency. Either way, the visual form serves as a powerful signifier of and vehicle for fears of the viewer.

It could be argued that certain commonly acknowledged constituents of the fear experience, such as being alone in the dark, away from helpful attachment figures and hearing a sudden, unidentifiable noise, are likely to be identified as such by so many people that they form a part of a 'collective unconscious'. This phrase was coined by C.G. Jung and is now considered in respect of the light it might shed on an understanding of fear.

C.G. Jung: the collective unconscious and the shadow

In addition to believing in a personal unconscious Jung believed that people were also subject to the influences of a 'collective' unconscious, i.e. an unconscious shared collectively by a group or particular culture. Fordham (1966, p.27) explains:

> The most direct expression of the collective unconscious is to be found when the archetypes, as primordial images, appear in dreams, unusual states of mind, or psychotic fantasies...the unconscious is the source of consciousness and of the creative and destructive spirit of mankind.

Whereas the personal unconscious will include that which is particular to an individual the collective unconscious comprises experiences that have been commonly shared by all peoples over centuries of evolution and development. These experiences are manifest in archetypal images found in creative arts, religious beliefs and mythologies and include peoples' struggles to understand and master their fears. One frequently recurring archetype was named 'the shadow' by Jung. Fordham (1966, p.49) writes:

The shadow is the inferior being in ourselves, the one who wants to do all the things that we do not allow ourselves to do, who is everything that we are not, the Mr Hyde to our Dr Jekyll. We have an inkling of this foreign personality when, after being possessed by an emotion or overcome with rage, we excuse ourselves by saying, 'I was not myself' or 'I really don't know what came over me'. What 'came over' was in fact the shadow, the primitive, uncontrolled and animal part of ourselves. The shadow also personifies itself when we particularly dislike someone, especially if it is an unreasonable dislike, we should suspect that we are actually disliking a quality of our own which we find in the other person.

The shadow therefore comprises the less acknowledged, less well-developed aspects of our selves. This is why it is commonly portrayed as deformed and/or disabled as Mr Hyde was. It is regarded by the individual with a mixture of hatred, contempt, envy and admiration; a projection of both what is despised and what is desired. Recognition of the shadow is particularly important to an understanding of fear as we tend to cast onto the scapegoat shadow aspects of ourselves that we do not fully comprehend and/or which we do not like. This applies equally to workers in health and social care and the service users they work with.

Mental health professionals might project their own 'madness' into service users they work with. Workers in youth offending teams might rid themselves of their own criminal tendencies in similar fashion. Colleagues could be seen as being outrageously unreasonable. Service user parents might project harsh, over-authoritarian aspects of themselves into workers undertaking child-protection tasks. Society generally can rid itself of responsibility for children who are killed by those who care for them by conducting an inquiry and blaming social workers and other professionals, exonerating itself from guilt and blame. Essentially the projection of the shadow into others offers a convenient way of ridding ourselves of our fears and absolving ourselves of blame. 'How come *they* are so controlling/perverse/irresponsible?' we might ask, secure in the knowledge that *we* would *never* be found guilty of such a charge.

Zweig and Abrams (1991, p.xx) reflect on the functioning of the shadow in the collective unconscious:

> While most individuals and groups live out the socially acceptable side of life, others seem to live out primarily the socially disowned parts. When

they become the object of negative group projections, the collective shadow takes the form of scapegoating, racism and enemy-making. To anti-Communist Americans, the USSR is the evil empire. To Moslems, America is the great Satan. To Nazis, the Jews are vermin Bolsheviks. To ascetic Christian monks, witches are in league with the devil. To South African advocates of apartheid or American members of the Ku Klux Klan, blacks are subhuman, undeserving of the rights and privileges of whites.

It is helpful for workers in health and social care to recognize that there are some people into whom they will be tempted to project their shadow side, just as they will particularly appeal to some others as a receptacle for their projections. Many workers have had the feeling at times that they are dealing with something considerably greater and more complex than the issues apparently under consideration. Quite possibly they are. Jung's concepts of the collective unconscious and the shadow help us to begin to understand what these 'greater presences' might be.

Jung suggests that a way forward when contending with these difficult forces is that we should get to know our own shadow better and take back our projections so that we can own that we, as well as others, have unpalatable and unpleasant aspects to our lives. This entails a preparedness to see others differently, less fearfully, to allow for the:

> ...realisation that the people living on the other side of the mountain are not made up exclusively of red-headed devils responsible for all of the evil on this side of the mountain. (C.G Jung quoted in Zweig and Abrams 1991, p.194)

Having outlined and considered some of the culturally induced filters through which we see our fears, after the recommendations for practice and training which end this chapter, the following chapters provide examples of fears encountered by health and social care workers engaged with different service user groups and discuss ways in which these fears were responded to.

Recommendations for practice and training

- Workers should be aware of the fundamental ambivalence which accompanies learning about fears in early childhood. Terrifying fears can be communicated soothingly and lovingly by way of nursery rhymes. Frightening fairy tales show the child that adversity can be overcome.

- The tension for health and social care workers needing to 'pursue' service users and discover things about them without over-reaching in the process should be acknowledged as constituting an intrinsic dynamic to the work.

- The fact that fears can be sought, welcomed and paid for as well as uncomfortable and distressing should be recognized.

- The importance of the visual image as a predominant signifier of fear needs appreciating but so too does the fact that workers might be more frightened by what they *do not* see and *do not* experience than by what they do.

- Fears should be accepted as originating from a 'collective' unconscious as well as a personal unconscious.

- The role of the shadow should be respected. Workers need to recognize that they might project their shadow characteristics onto/into colleagues and service users at times. At other times they will be a receptacle for the unacknowledged and unwanted shadows of those they work with and for.

Chapter 2

Child Care and Child Protection Work in Community Settings

Introduction

This chapter begins with evidence of how fear is considered ambivalently in government inquiries into child deaths. On the one hand, the profound and paralysing influences of fears on professional judgement and practice are acknowledged and understood. On the other hand, workers seem to be expected to make sound judgements regardless of the disabling effects of their fears. Examples are given of workers being threatened by service users and possible responses to these threats are considered. The influence of the imagination in embellishing and enlarging fears is illustrated and the inner 'reality' of these experiences acknowledged. Extreme circumstances in which fear can kill people because of what they believe are highlighted and discussed. Fears of physical assault and fears of losing control are also considered. The debate as to whether fears are more potent and influential when coming from inside or outside of the individual is a focus throughout the chapter and the predominantly future-orientated nature of fear is apparent.

Fear and inquiries into child deaths

In the UK there have now been more than 30 inquiries into child deaths since the death of Maria Colwell in 1974 and 19 of these have been summarized by the Department of Health (1991). Fear is a feature of many of these reports and yet its existence is acknowledged with the ambivalence typically characteristic of responses to fears which is highlighted in Chapter One. Writing of the death of Kimberley Carlile:

> The inquiry considered that 'how the team leader failed to see the blindingly obvious [severe physical and emotional abuse] is explicable only by the fact that he was blinded by his incompetence in assessing child deception by abusing parents, something all social workers must be constantly alive to. (Department of Health 1991, p.69)

This is an interestingly worded claim. The inquiry finds only one possible explanation for the team leader (Martin Ruddock) not seeing abuse – his incompetence. It also claims that this explanation is not one possible explanation among several but that it is *the* only one, indeed that it transcends all opinion or conjecture and achieves the status of 'fact'. However, there are several other possible explanations as to why the team leader may not have seen the abuse: fear, for one. In an aptly entitled paper, 'When fear blinds the mind's eye', Marijana (1996) shows how the capacity of professionals to recognize (see) difficulties inherent in their work can be obscured and obstructed by fear. The inquiry's use of the phrase 'blindingly obvious' is interesting in this respect!

In a rare published response to being criticized in a child death inquiry Ruddock (1998, p.93) argues back, 'At its crudest this chapter is about whether I was an excuse-giving, bumbling idiot or whether job pressure and its resulting stress undermined my ability, and a service's ability, to intervene to save Kimberley Carlile.' He refers to the inquiry's comment that his submission to them 'is not only an outstanding document of insight into a social worker's tasks. But it is also well written, movingly reflective and self critically analytical. It avoids casting blame on others, in circumstances where it might have been expected' (Ruddock 1998, p.94). Not so much of the blinded and incompetent professional here!

The Carlile inquiry also acknowledges other factors at work that could have contributed to Kimberley's death:

> We suspect the team leader was overworked to the detriment of his professionalism…(with) high turnover of staff, unfilled vacancies, inexperience among newly promoted managers and with longer serving ones at the end of their tether, the climate becomes one of siege. (Quoted in Department of Health 1991, p.36)

Given that these additional factors are acknowledged by the same inquiry it is interesting that they should single out incompetence as being the *only* possible reason for Ruddock not seeing the abuse.

The Department of Health mention fear explicitly in relation to Nigel Hall, a service user with a reputation for violence:

> Social services and school staff found Nigel Hall intimidating. The effects of fear of violence are likely very hard to identify... It is not easy to admit to being afraid... We encourage social workers to...speak out if they are fearful for their own safety or if they consider their performance as a social worker is being handicapped by fear of violence. (Department of Health 1991, p.71)

This appears to be a helpful acknowledgement of the very real and disabling effects fear can have on a social worker's judgement and performance. However, the extract continues, '...anger, aggressive and destructive behaviour and the possibility of violent impulsive reactions should be faced. The social worker needs to maintain an open, structured relationship with the family.' This appears to suggest that social workers should have faced whatever anger there was. It also implies that families can be worked with by way of an 'open, structured relationship'. However, the nature and extent of cruelty, violence, sadism and torture documented in these inquiries by adults in positions of care and trust almost defies belief at times. It does not seem likely that such people can be safely and constructively engaged within the confines of an open, structured relationship.

The Carlile inquiry states:

> Two social workers visited and were told by the parents that the children were in bed. The inquiry considered that despite the determined resistance the workers might have said in not so many words we are not leaving until we have seen the two younger children. (Department of Health 1991, p.77)

In expressing this opinion no concern whatsoever is shown for the safety or wellbeing of the social workers concerned. Those working in health and social care settings will often need to face and deal with people they know to be potentially violent or extremely dangerous. Many workers have been threatened (Stanley and Goddard 2002) and some have been killed by service users they have worked with (Norris 1990; Reith 1998). Despite this the Carlile inquiry considers that the workers should have stood their ground and refused to leave before seeing the children. Such action could have been indefensible under the terms of the Health and Safety at Work Act 1974 which charges each employee to engage with their work responsibly and safely. Yes, the children needed protection but so too did the workers.

A more useful suggestion could have been for the workers to have spoken of their fears to their seniors as advocated in relation to Nigel Hall (above) and to have been supported in safe working practices by their employers exercising their duty of care. If a follow-up visit was agreed upon the social workers could have returned accompanied and supported by the police. Fear is a protective mechanism that can help to keep people safe and alive. To ignore it or dismiss it too quickly with too little thought is, ultimately, not in our interests.

A later publication by the Department of Health (1995) warns of fear of a different kind:

> We must not pretend that actions taken by child protection agencies can ever guarantee that parents will not harm their children. The danger of trying to give such guarantees and of pillorying those agencies when harm does occur is that inappropriate interventions may be made out of fear. (Department of Health 1995, p.i)

Here the Department of Health is recognizing that if social workers and others are constantly reproached for not doing enough to protect children fears of this criticism may prove counter-productive and lead to over-reaction. It is an adage that social workers are 'damned if they do (remove children from their parents or carers) and damned if they do not'. Having removed children after suspected sexual abuse in Cleveland in 1987 social workers were criticized for being over-zealous and insufficiently aware of the extent to which parents and carers loved and cared for their children. When children have died at the hands of their parents or carers social workers have subsequently been criticized for being unduly optimistic about the nature and extent of the love that parents and carers have for their children and naïve as to the cultural norms through which this love is expressed (London Borough of Brent 1985). Those working in health and social care can often find themselves caught between the dual fears of being insufficiently vigilant in relation to the true nature and extent of abuse by those they are involved with and being insufficiently tolerant of symptoms and signs that are 'known but not fully appreciated, or, not fitting the current mode of understanding' (Department of Health 1991, pp.58–60).

A different kind of fear again is referred by La Fontaine in her inquiry into the extent and nature of organised and ritual sexual abuse of children. She writes:

> While the children were said over and over again to be exhibiting strange terrors which defied rational explanation, what created an equally strong impression but went unremarked was the fear they induced in the professionals who dealt with them. (Department of Health 1995, p.73)

Working with children and adults who have made claims of being ritually abused by those forming part of a Satanist network has provoked fear of particular potency and intensity in the caring professions (Cook and Kelly 1997; Sinason 1994). Once again the fears influence and shape what can be believed and what cannot. Professionals were said to be divided between 'believers' and 'sceptics' (Nursten and Smith 1996) each fighting for what they saw to be in the best interests of children who may be at risk. Sometimes children are abused in ways and to an extent that seem 'beyond belief' and, knowing this, professionals may therefore come to regard any form of perversion, depravity and sadism as possible and in need of guarding against. La Fontaine's view was that a belief in Satanic practices provided a context within which abuse could be conceptualized. This may have afforded some comfort to professionals but stigmatized (usually lower-class and less powerful) innocent people:

> Some [professionals] were so deeply shocked that they were prepared to accept the suggestion…that the acts they heard described were characteristic of Satanism and ritualism. In order to reconcile themselves to an intractable abuse case they strayed into the territory of romance – and in the process demonised the marginal poor. (Department of Health 1995, p.73)

Fear also features in the inquiry into the death of Ainlee Labonte in Newham in 2002. The police were frequently called to respond to domestic violence incidents and health visitors and housing officers would not make home visits as a consequence of the threats and violence they had previously been subjected to. Ainlee's mother's partner was removed from a general practitioner's list because of abusive behaviour and medical records relating to Ainlee were stolen from a hospital. The police experience of Ainlee's mother and her partner was that they were 'a violent, aggressive, obstructive, devious and dishonest couple' (Newham Area Child Protection Committee 2002, p.22). The inquiry notes, 'The fear with which the family are regarded leads to almost paralysis in terms of action' (Newham Area Child Protection Committee 2002, p.18).

Responses to fear are typically fight, flight or freezing. The organizational 'paralysis' referred to here brings to mind the image of the rabbit, caught in the car headlights, frozen by fear. Freezing in response to fear has been seen as a useful survival mechanism in some instances as if an animal suspects a predator may be in the bushes, then to keep still, make no sound and thus avoid detection may save the animal's life. However, for the rabbit caught in the headlights the freezing may lead to its death. Paralysis as a result of fear could contribute to continuing life or ending it, depending on the context. It is a response frequently observable from both organizations and individuals as will become apparent from the case studies cited in this book.

A recommendation of many inquiries is that appropriate training should be made available for those in the caring professions to equip them to deal with these extremely difficult and disturbing situations. However, the nature and extent of cruelty and abuse shown in these inquiries portrays almost 'inhuman' behaviour. A fundamental (and probably unanswerable) question for those in the caring professions is how can human beings engage and work with those engaging in inhuman behaviours? The scale and complexity of this difficulty has been acknowledged recently by the Department of Health:

> There's a tendency to translate a rather big issue into something that can be measured and ticked because of all the frenzy about outcomes at the moment. In one case when there was serious intimidation the Department of Health sent out messages saying 'you must be careful about parents who intimidate or lie' and 'what are you going to do about it?' Social workers need to be helped through this but the sort of thing you get is a proposal for a few days' awareness training, as if you could just de-intimidate social workers. It's ludicrous. (Department of Health 2002, p.43)

It is far easier to ask 'what are you going to do about it?' than answer this question. There are no straightforward, quick-fix answers and yet responses need to be made to the tragic deaths of children at the hands of those entrusted with their care and careful thought given as to how such deaths might be prevented. The typical 'Never again!' headlines in tabloid newspapers following child deaths have appeared too frequently to have credibility. A deeper and more sympathetic understanding of the difficulties faced by those charged with the responsibility of protecting children is called for. Careful descriptions and analysis of fears faced by these workers is a place to start. Experiences of fear related by those working in child care/child protection roles in community settings now follow beginning with fears arising from being threatened and fears of physical assault.

Fears of threats and of the imagination 'running riot'

A social worker, working in Northern Ireland, related the following:

> I was moving a baby from hospital just after the mother had given birth. The baby's father and his brother were there also. They became abusive and threatening. The police were there to help me move the baby. The baby's uncle had threatened to follow to where the baby was to be placed and cause havoc. I was in a lift with a policeman who had a gun and the uncle was waiting at the bottom floor where the lift stopped. I was having to make a run for the car with the baby and was feeling very vulnerable... The family had a well-known history with the police and social services so the threats were real and I could imagine them carrying them out. The threats were to punch me, 'deal with' us, shoot us.

This quotation describes one of the most difficult and painful aspects of a social worker's job – that of removing a baby from its mother. Social workers need to know that there is good evidence for this course of action and feel justified in what they are doing. However, even with evidence and justification, it is a heart-wrenching act to have to perform. Support from the police had been arranged as difficulties had been anticipated and the possibility of injury, or even death, was apparent from the policeman's gun and the threats that the worker would be shot. The phrase, 'the threats were real' is an interesting one as threats, by their nature, are not about what has happened (the real) but about what may happen in the future (the not-yet-known). By using this phrase the worker is conveying that she thought it quite possible, even likely, that the people making the threats would act on them and turn them into reality.

How best to respond to threats is a question many workers in health and social care have asked themselves from time to time. Workers have been threatened with guns to their heads, with screwdrivers, ashtrays, chairs, knives and car bombs. They have also been subject to threats of sexual assault, been followed to their home and told that their children are at risk (Stanley and Goddard 2002). There is the possibility of sharing these threats with the police. 'Threats to kill' is an offence that people can be charged with. However, not every threat will be seen as a chargeable offence and discretion is exercised by the police in terms of how 'seriously' they will take the threat. There is also the possibility that 'attention feeds' and that by giving time and thought to the threat this very process makes fulfilment of the threat more likely than it may otherwise have been. On the other hand, threats need to be taken seriously…

De Becker advises:

> How one responds to a threat determines whether it will be a valuable instrument or mere words…the listener and not the speaker decides how powerful a threat will be… Even in cases in which threats are determined to be serious we advise clients never to show the threatener a high appraisal of his words, never to show fear. (De Becker 1997, p.109)

The notion that it is the hearer, and not the speaker, of a threat who determines the power of that threat is an interesting one, and not readily obvious. It suggests that the person making the threat may need a response to their threat before they know how powerful it may be. There can sometimes be a sense in which emotions need *fuelling* in order to survive and continue much as a fire needs oxygen. An angry response to an angry stimulus is likely to escalate the extent of anger generated whereas a calm response is likely to modify the anger. If someone persistently refuses to be frightened by another person's intimidation then the would-be intimidator will eventually realize that the effect desired from their behaviour is not forthcoming. This is why De Becker's advice is never to show fear even when it may be felt.

Some threats are easier to ignore than others. One female participant, speaking of a male service user, said, 'He said he was going to get me, beat me up, follow me home… I would be sorry…the threats were against *me*, not against the department…' The fact that she distinguished the threat as being directed against her rather than the department suggests that the man had succeeded in breaching her defences and making her feel vulnerable and exposed on a personal rather than a professional level.

Others, usually managers, supervisors and seniors, under-estimating or not acknowledging the profound impact of experiences of stress and fear on workers was reported as being the most unhelpful response to these experiences in both research projects written of here. Most threats are not acted upon and much of what is feared by workers does not materialize. A manager, being removed from the immediate context of the threat and not having been exposed to it, may therefore be both less aware of the extent of its impact and more preoccupied with other things. He may say, 'Well, let's wait and see what happens – it will probably come to nothing anyway', or, 'Well, nothing actually happened, did it?' Whilst both of these statements may be true they deny the fact that in the mind of the person threatened or frightened something considerable *has* happened.

People can bring about changes in their heart rate and body temperature by merely imagining things, for example when listening to an erotic description (Sapolsky 1998, p.19). Real changes can therefore be brought about by something that is not real. In the instances when workers feel slighted and discounted by the 'nothing happened' response from managers they are literally speaking from different realities. Workers would agree that nothing has happened in the 'real' outer world yet be acutely aware that things had happened inside their heads with all of the forcefulness of the most real-seeming nightmare. Fears are subjectively perceived and experienced and it is sometimes the case that one person's most dreaded fear is seen by another person as a challenge to be relished. A manager hearing about a fear may therefore regard what he hears as fairly innocuous and it would be very difficult for the person experiencing the fear to show it to be otherwise, particularly in the limited time that workers often have to explain things to their busy managers. Sometimes the worker herself may regard her fear as being more deeply resonant than the situation merits and yet still be left to deal with the impact of that fear. An example of this from my own personal experience is given in Chapter One and the following quotation from a female field social worker participant also shows this process at work. She is recalling a visit made to a residential children's home when a situation got out of hand:

The children were aged in between five and thirteen. I do not remember how many there were, in my darkest thoughts I seem to think there were dozens of them, but there could only have been seven or eight.

The way in which this memory is expressed is illustrative as, when relating it, the worker shows herself to be aware of at least two different ways in which she remembers what happened. On the one hand there are her 'darkest thoughts' in which dozens of children are present. On the other is her rational awareness which tells her that, in fact, there were only seven or eight children. One of the difficulties affecting workers who have experienced fears and those trying to help them to deal with the impact of these fears is that there is often a 'darkest thoughts' response to incidents as well as a more rational, consciously accurate response. Workers may know the 'darkest thoughts' response to be inaccurate and potentially unhelpful and yet be profoundly influenced by it nonetheless. In the research into distress the second most mentioned immediate impact of distressing experiences reported by participants after fear was that of the imagination 'running riot'. The expression is revealing as participants know that their fears are imaginary rather than real. They also know that their imagination is 'blowing their fears up, out of all proportion' and yet they are still left needing to deal with these fears in all of their real-seeming force. The fact that fears are often used to construct a version of a possible future means they can never be conclusively disproved or out-argued. Another example of the imagination 'running riot' in response to a fear-provoking possibility is provided by a participant who had visited some young children who had been jumping on some pit bull terrier dogs that did not appear to be well trained, pushing and pulling them. She recalls:

> I would see visual images of the dogs turning on the children…dripping jaws and a lot of blood. I had seen a bedroom where the dogs had been left alone and they had ripped up a mattress – this did not help the images.

A fascinating question about the nature of fear turns on whether fears are more potent in relation to stimuli 'outside' people or as a result of the disturbing scenarios they create by way of their imagination 'inside' themselves. This is an important question as fear can actually kill people as Sargant explains, writing of 'hex' (voodoo or psycho-physiological) death:

> The power of the witch-doctor is very great in some regions…those who really believe in this power can actually die of fear, just as people in the West can die of fear when their basic terrors are aroused… The victim may become so frightened that he goes into a state of acute anxiety, in which most of the bodily secretions and metabolic functions are severely disturbed: secretions essential to life are dried up by fear, and he eventually dies of fright physiologically. (Sargant 1973, p.122)

Martin provides a recent example of people dying as a result of their fears for the future:

> During the Gulf War of 1991 Iraq launched a series of missile attacks against Israel. Many Israeli civilians died as a result of these attacks. But the vast majority of them did not die from any direct physical effects of the missiles. They died from the heart failure brought on by the fear, anxiety and stress associated with the bombardment. They died because of what was going on in their minds… The 'extra' deaths were concentrated in areas of Israel where the levels of fear and anxiety were highest. (Martin 1997, p.3)

This extract shows how fear-fuelled imagination may be a more dangerous killer than bombs. It therefore suggests that fears are more likely to be fatal when 'inside' individuals than when outside them. In doing so it provides further reasons as to why individuals' responses to fears should never be minimized or discounted, however extreme or implausible-sounding and whatever the outer, 'real-world' reality. Most workers in health and social care will not be called upon to respond professionally to situations involving hex death and bombs; they are far more likely to have to deal with fears that they may be physically assaulted. However, even when being assaulted the fears often most potently recalled are not relating to what is happening or what has happened but what may yet happen. Once again, the 'shaping spirit' of imagination can be seen to be at work.

Fears of physical assault

A female social worker in a children and families team related the following experience:

> I was in a meeting with a woman who had two of her children in foster care and the other two in the care of their father. She had problems as the

result of drug and alcohol abuse. The purpose of the meeting was to let her know that there were no plans to return the children home to her and she took exception to this. She stormed out of the room and kicked a bin. I went after her to help her to get a speedy exit out of the building. She couldn't have left on her own as there was a security door. In the reception area she leapt on me. She had me by the hair and was swinging me around. She then got me on the ground and kicked my nose and fractured my tooth. I'm paranoid about my teeth and when she kicked me in the teeth I wondered what damage might have been done. She then started swinging a plant pot around. My fear was of what damage she might do, and that she wasn't going to stop. The receptionists were watching through a glass dividing door and I was aware of them being there... I felt embarrassment. It was a bit of a spectacle... She was known to have been verbally abusive previously but not physically violent and out of all the workers I was the one who would be said to have the good relationship with her. After the incident was over she went to the police station and said that she had assaulted her social worker.

Even in this situation when a service user had already injured and hurt a worker the worker's predominantly remembered fear was not about what had been done to her but what the service user may yet go on to do, '...my fear was of what damage she might do...' The limitations of risk assessment are exposed as the worker shows that the violent service user had not been assessed as being high risk and, in any event, the worker she assaulted was the one thought to have the best relationship with her.

It is ironic that the 'security' door installed in order to afford workers safety and protection actually serves precisely the opposite function and contributes to the very outcome that it is intended to prevent. If the service user did not need accompanying to be let out of the door she might have been able to leave more promptly on her own terms and the assault on the worker might not have happened. Sometimes 'security' doors and 'panic' alarms appear to be useful and pragmatic responses to fears. However, careful thought should be given before installing these devices and their use must be carefully rehearsed in order to help ensure that they do not bring about more harm than good.

The worker's recollection of the receptionists watching through a glass dividing door is an example of the separation from potentially helpful attachment figures highlighted as being so important to experiences of fear by Bowlby (1973, 1988) and first mentioned in Chapter One. Being unable to reach or be reached by attachment figures is shown to be a recurring theme of crucial importance in many participants' accounts of their fears. Again, a door, which could provide a helpful entrance to a safe place, is remembered as serving the opposite function of a barrier instead. The worker's mention of embarrassment and of providing 'a bit of a spectacle' is also interesting. Several participants spoke of a feeling of embarrassment or foolishness as a response to an experience of fear. One wonders why they should feel this, particularly, when they had often done little or nothing to provoke the situation in the first place. The words speak of self-consciousness in relation to performance. Literature relating to role theory (Goffman [1959] 1978), script theory (Berne 1975) and drama therapy (Jennings 1997; Jennings and Minde 1993) aids understanding of the feelings of 'playing a part' which may characterize fear-provoking experiences.

The fact that the service user is remembered as having gone to tell the police about what she had done could be read in two different ways. She may have been sorry and remorseful for assaulting the worker or she may have wanted to tell her version of events first and thought it would be better for her were she to volunteer this information. The two possibilities are not mutually exclusive.

Participants' accounts of fears often included several different fears which overlapped, inter-twined and operated on different levels at the same time. The experience just discussed included both fears arising from being physically assaulted when working in a child care setting and fears of an incident getting out of control. The next two fears related highlight fears of losing control as their predominant theme.

Fears of losing control

A social worker, working in a hospital setting, recalled:

> I had set up a visit on a hospital ward for some children to come in to see someone who had been a very caring father. The kids were excited and he was looking forward to it but I hadn't realized that his mental state had rapidly deteriorated and there had been no warning of this from the ward. He became very threatening and called them little whores. The kids were being absolutely destroyed. I felt that I was going to be hit. It was a terribly destructive experience for those girls.

Fears often surface and make themselves known when people think they are dealing with one thing only to suddenly and unexpectedly find that they are, in fact, dealing with something else entirely. Bettelheim (1979) suggests that children are most frightened by fairy stories when they discover that a person they had thought to be good turns out to be bad. It is the sudden, unanticipated transformation that inspires the fear. In the example just described the social worker, father and children were all looking forward to his visit but it unexpectedly turned out to be quite different from what was expected. The worker conveys a sense of 'everything going wrong' in a catastrophic sense. The kids were 'destroyed', he feared that he would be assaulted. Instead of the keenly anticipated happy reunion the visit turned out to be 'terribly destructive'. The worker describes himself as having seen himself to be in a controlling position of influence and of setting something up with all good intentions. Suddenly, he finds the reality quite different to that which he had perceived it to be. This left him feeling overwhelmed and out of control: a helpless, hapless onlooker forced to watch the children he had wanted to please being 'destroyed' by the chain of events that he had set in motion.

Sometimes workers described experiences of fear with a surreal, 'uncanny' (Royle 2003) sense of cinematic recall:

> I was asked to deliver a letter to a client. My knock on the door was answered by a client who was drunk, then another client came down who was also drunk. He asked, 'What do you want?' and was talking a load of rubbish. I asked after the child and was told that she was sleeping. I said, 'Can I see the child?' and the child's father came to the stairs and said, 'Come on in.' I wasn't really sure of what I should be doing. In the room were six people, five of which were in different levels of intoxication. Again, I asked to see the child. I was getting a lot of sexualized innuendo, sexualized talk. I thought, 'What am I doing in this flat? I should have got someone to come with me.' Someone came out of a bedroom. I was afraid that I would get raped. I went up to the child's bedroom. There was more sexualized talk. The child was whimpering and clutching a pound coin. On seeing me it rushed to me and clung to me.

Stepping through the doorway it seems as if the social worker has entered another world where disinhibition is facilitated by the use of alcohol and normal rules do not apply. The invitation to 'Come on in' is reminiscent of encouragements in fairy tales where the protagonist's fate is decided by how she responds. Almost immediately the worker finds herself disorientated and unsure of herself: 'I wasn't really sure of what I should be doing… I thought, "What am I doing in this flat?"' whereas just a few minutes previously she would have claimed to know the purpose of her visit. This is another example of the fear that arises from a sudden and unexpected change. Sometimes workers were not sure of the precise reason for their fear but this worker was – she mentions fear of rape rather than fear of other physical assault, losing control or anything else she could have mentioned. Stairs, bedrooms, sleeping and sex feature a number of times in her account and these features provide the context for her memory. Despite her fear she continues to the child's bedroom. The pound coin has poignancy but its meaning or relevance is not clear. This contributes to the simultaneous clarity and lack of clarity of what is described.

This participant's account encapsulates most of the main categories of fear which emerged from the research. While the fear of sexual assault predominates this entails the accompanying likelihood of physical assault. There is the fear of being overwhelmed by, and losing control of, a situation that one has set in motion along with the fears of separation from attachment figures that could be helpful. Fears do not fit into neat, well-organized little boxes but merge, blend and co-mingle with one another. Nevertheless, certain themes can be seen to recur through workers' experiences of fear and, following recommendations for practice and training, these are next considered in relation to, and arising from, mental health work.

Recommendations for practice and training

- Ways in which fear can 'blind the mind's eye' should be accorded greater recognition in inquiries into child deaths and workers should be blamed less for being too fearful to think properly.

- The potentially corrosive influence of constant criticism and blame on workers' morale should be appreciated.

- Societal and structural responsibility for child deaths should be admitted as well as individuals being singled out for blame.

- The difficulty, if not impossibility, of working openly and positively with some families should be accepted.

- The right of workers to be free from violence and threats of violence when undertaking their duties should be upheld.

- Workers should guard against the dangers of being unduly optimistic (and insufficiently fearful) in relation to those they work with.

- Allowance should be made for the possible emergence of new fears not fitting current modes of understanding.

- Organizational paralysis in the face of extreme fears should be guarded against.

- Some training that helps workers to identify and respond to their fears might be helpful but the limitations of such training should also be accepted given the multi-faceted and extremely complex nature of some risks encountered and the fears these give rise to.

- The potentially disabling nature of some threats made to workers should be appreciated.

- Workers should be aware of the extent to which their responses (or lack of them) to threats might determine the potency of such threats.

- Managers and supervisors should acknowledge the potential impact of threats on workers even when these are not carried out.

- The power of imagination when workers 'fear the worst' should be respected – people can die as a consequence of being afraid.

- Perceived positive relationships with service users should not be regarded as a safeguard against being attacked.

- Devices installed to promote safer working should be recognized also as potentially increasing danger in the wrong circumstances.

- Shame and embarrassment arising from perceived poor performance should be acknowledged as frequent attendants of workers' fears.

- Suddenly and unexpectedly changing situations should be recognized as profoundly fear-provoking.

- The place of the surreal and the 'uncanny' in the fear experience should be respected.

Chapter 3

Mental Health Work

Introduction

This chapter begins with a consideration of whether fears are more potent when coming from outside of the individual (fears of separation) or from inside (fears of annihilation). Fears of workers' imaginations running riot are then illustrated. Ways in which a service user may force himself into the mind of a worker are shown as are fears that a worker might experience for his family and home life as well as himself. The difficulties and fear-provoking consequences of working with those who have abused drugs or alcohol and who suffer mental illness are recognized. The importance of the eyes as transmitters of fear and the intuition as a protective mechanism when feeling fearful are highlighted. The strange yet deep sense of protection that workers may feel when exposed to trauma is illustrated as is the tendency for people to forget what they know when fearful. The relevance of the 'drama triangle' to fearful states is shown as people may move rapidly between roles of victim, persecutor and rescuer. The importance of the 'hero myth' in the motivation of many workers in health and social care settings is suggested. The three main possible responses to fear – fight, flight or freezing – are illustrated. The profound and long-lasting impacts of fearful experiences along with a cinematic capacity for recall of detail are apparent throughout all accounts.

Fears of separation and annihilation

Reference has been made in previous chapters to Bowlby's (1973) contention that fear of separation is the worst imaginable fear for human beings.

Bowlby claims that men and women are essentially social animals and need connectedness with one another in order to survive and to flourish. Cut off from the group people are vulnerable to danger and prone to fear:

> Probably nothing increases the likelihood that fear will be aroused more than [being alone]. Finding oneself alone in a strange place, perhaps in darkness, and met by a sudden movement or mysterious sound, few of us would be unafraid. Were we to have with us even one stout companion, however, we should probably feel much braver; and given many our courage would quickly return. Being alone, like conscience, 'doth make cowards of us all'. (Bowlby 1973, pp.118–119)

To face a threat in the company of others is likely to inspire less fear than the prospect of facing the same threat alone. From his analysis of fairy tales Bettelheim (1979) concurs with Bowlby that fear of separation is the worst fear of all:

> There is no greater threat in life than that we will be deserted, left all alone. Psychoanalysis has named this – man's greatest fear – separation anxiety and the younger we are, the more excruciating is our anxiety when we feel deserted, for the young child actually perishes when not adequately protected and taken care of. (Bettelheim 1979, p.145)

The extent to which Bowlby's ideas are central to the Department of Health's (2000) *Framework for the Assessment of Children in Need and their Families* is indicative of their current potency and popularity. A 'secure base' and secure attachments are considered necessary for stable mental health in children and in adults alike. Freud (1953) also initially regarded fears of separation as being the most difficult for human beings to face but he later modified this view and argued that the greatest threat came not from losing touch with others but from destructive forces at work within the individual. Having claimed originally that people were influenced primarily by the needs to satisfy the pleasure principle (*Eros*) Freud observed the impact of World War I and saw the extent of man's capacity for destruction. He therefore amended his views to posit also the existence of a 'death instinct' (*Thanatos*) (Freud 1955a). Freud's work on the death instinct was taken up by Klein [1946] (1988) who argued that people had more to fear from the operation of the death instinct within than from fears of separation from 'outside' relationships:

> I hold that anxiety arises from the operation of the death instinct within the organism, is felt as fear of annihilation (death) and takes the form of fear of persecution...the anxiety of being destroyed from within remains active...under the pressure of this threat the ego tends to fall to pieces. (Klein [1946] 1988, p.4)

For Klein internal persecutors are most to be feared. Unlike Bowlby she regarded the real, external world as representing a secondary cause of fear when compared to the tyrannical persecutory inner world of phantasy and destruction. Dockar-Drysdale (1990) supports Klein's view:

> The dread of emotional inner annihilation is infinitely more terrible than the objective fear of real death. Often, an extreme terror of death in children and grown ups alike covers the underlying dread of annihilation. We talk about 'separation anxiety' but this is often a euphemism to describe the fear of annihilation. Annihilation involves total destruction of the child and the whole universe. Of course the child will not really be objectively annihilated; but his dread is real. (Dockar-Drysadle 1990, p.55)

The contention that separation anxiety is a 'euphemism' is interesting, suggesting that this concept is more palatable than that of the 'death instinct' which we would prefer not to acknowledge. Even so, we recognize the truth that 'each man kills the thing he loves' (Wilde [1896] 1997, p.748), and know that people will sometimes cut off their nose to spite their face. Individuals do seem to have a 'self-destruct' button and at times be apparently driven to bring about their own downfall. The question of whether fears are more potent when 'outside' or 'inside' individuals was first raised in the previous chapter and will continue to be considered throughout this chapter as fears arising from mental health work are illustrated. Assessing likely danger is particularly problematic when working with threats and delusions as the imagination is prone to 'running riot' at such times.

Fears arising from the imagination 'running riot'

A social worker working in a community mental health team related the following:

> I was seeing a person who had been convicted of arson and assault. She made abusive phone calls and threats and kept letting me know that she

knew where I lived. I was afraid that something would happen to me, my home, or my family. She suffered depression and deliberately self-harmed. She had committed arson because others had not shared her beliefs about the rights of animals. She was saying, 'Do you know such and such a place? I know where you live.' I lived in the same town as her. She made phone calls to me at work, shouting abuse, blaming me for everything, talking about what she was going to do. Someone kept calling me at home and hanging up. I think that it was her. She kept driving up and down outside my office and getting hotel managers to call me when she was drunk to come and sort her out. She followed me in her car and would pull in to park just behind me, then she would suddenly speed past me. I felt she was trying to knock me down. The brakes failed on my car once and I feared that she had cut them. I asked the police to check. She hadn't, and it was a coincidence that they had failed. I think I had the problems because she had disclosed certain information to me about herself. I questioned my practice terribly. What had I done? I became hyper-vigilant at night. I was sleepless and had nightmares. I was constantly watching for her car. I knew her registration number and kept checking. In my dreams I was reliving events. I kept going over what had happened.

This worker describes how a service user's threats caused her to fear that she and/or her family were at risk. She knew the woman to be both a danger to herself, as she self-harmed, and to others, in that she had committed arson and assault. The threats intruded upon both the worker's home and place of work and thus made it difficult for the worker to maintain appropriate professional boundaries when thinking about them. The worker lived in the same town as the service user and knew that the service user knew where she lived. This compounded the difficulty of establishing and maintaining a professional distance. The service user's driving up and down outside the worker's office, following her in a car, and pulling in to park just behind her, are, in themselves, not abusive behaviours but could be intended and/or understood as such. Similarly, saying, 'I know where you live' is not, in itself, a threat but could be delivered or taken as one. This is why the worker's interpretation or 'reading' of the threat is crucial in determining its power (see the advice of De Becker (1997) in Chapter Two).

The service user seems to have forced her way into the mind of the worker as the worker suspects her when someone repeatedly calls on the telephone only to hang up. The worker questions herself, doubting her practice and becoming hyper-vigilant at night to the extent that she cannot sleep. Even when she is able to sleep the service user intrudes upon her dreams. The worker ruminates on events, obsessively. She fears the service user is trying to injure or kill her, by suddenly speeding past her and by cutting the brakes of her car. This account provides an example of the difficulty of determining whether fears are more potent in relation to 'outside' events in the 'real' world or as a result of the inner fears of annihilation which are activated by outside stimuli. It seems that the service user did not actually *do* anything to harm the worker. It is difficult to separate out what was actually threatened by the service user from that feared by the worker. When a 'reality check' was provided by the police checking the worker's brakes the service user was found not to have caused their failure. Whether it comes primarily from 'inside' or 'outside' of the worker and however (un)realistic her appraisal of the threat may be, the worker's sense of fear is palpable and therefore needs to acknowledged as such.

A further example of difficulty in ascertaining the potential extent of a threat is provided by a nurse counselling a service user experiencing problems with drug and alcohol abuse:

> My fear is of some clients' states of mind and the ideas that they are formulating. These are thoughts and ideas that you can't reason with by argument and penetration of evidence. Sometimes people with paranoid thoughts and ideas have been describing events outside of the session which they then bring into the session. One client had this idea that people outside were either in the blues or the blacks. People fell into two separate camps. He put himself in the black camp and attributed all kinds of negative attributes to those in the blues. The question then came around as to whether I was in the blues or the blacks. You're then trying to put across you're in neither, but according to his reckoning everyone's either in the blues or the blacks and the whole thing is spiralling downwards and your explanation can never be satisfactory. Suddenly it's in the room. It's come alive and you're having this debate about which camp you're in. The only way I can describe it physically, it feels like detachment... I'm there, but I'm not there, like I'm looking through a camera...there's a detachment, there's intrigue in it, what's going on? The whole atmosphere, and their eyes and your eyes, and they're looking into your eyes as if they might see something there which tells them whether you're a black or a blue... At the same time there's the feeling,

'What's going on outside?', I can't believe it stops here. This must be very strange for the person on the street... It doesn't make you any safer but it's a comfortable feeling – that whatever happens you'll come to no harm.

This participant shows how frightening it is to be caught up in someone else's delusion in the knowledge that all of one's usually-relied-upon powers of persuasion and argument will be of no use. Such difficulties characterize much work conducted with people suffering mental illness and those who have abused alcohol and/or drugs. The thoughts from outside of the session suddenly come alive in the room, in the moment. Attempts to avoid categorization are useless. The worker has to be a blue or a black. It is interesting to note that this participant begins by talking about himself in the first person but part way through his account moves out of this and continues using the second person. This tendency was apparent in the accounts of a number of participants interviewed and represents a way of speakers putting distance between themselves and their experience as they relate it. As if they do not want to stay too close to the fears as they are remembering them.

This sense of creating distance is also apparent from the way in which the participant goes on to talk of his sense of detachment, 'I'm there but I'm not there, like I'm looking through a camera...' In his mind's eye the participant moves from being the observer of this disturbing behaviour to observing himself in his role. He withdraws even further, as he continues with his account, to considering the perspective of the person on the street, thereby getting further and further away from being in the room with the service user. The participant also draws attention to the significance of the eyes in non-verbal communication, recalling the notion that the eyes are the mirrors of the soul, and contain within them the truth which is sought.

Despite the fear felt by the worker and conveyed in his account he feels comfortable that, although in danger, he will be safe and 'come to no harm'. This could be a long-established message of secure attachment from childhood, represent an existential/religious belief, or be a denial of the extent of danger he was truly in. It was interesting that, when under threat, some participants talked of a strange and yet resonant feeling of being pro-tected at the time while others recalled the opposite feeling, that they were 'doomed' or 'done for'. At least this service user told the participant what was on/in his mind and thereby made the material available for discussion of sorts by bringing it out into the open. Although these ideas were frightening to hear, perhaps the fact that the service user was willing to share them with the worker made them less dangerous. It may be that workers are at greater risk when service users entertain thoughts such as these and do not voice them but act on them instead.

As with the social worker quoted above this worker had reason to be fearful and found his imagination suggesting disconcerting possibilities. Because he recalled a single event rather than a sequence, however, perhaps he was able to keep his concerns about the potential danger in check more than the previously quoted worker who needed to deal with a number of distressing possibilities over a period of time.

Having considered examples of fears which were particularly potent because of workers' imaginations 'running riot', I will now discuss fears of death arising from mental health work.

Fears of death

In the account which follows a social worker describes another incident when 'nothing happened' in the 'real' world but a great deal happened in her mind:

> I was working in a psychiatric unit with a schizophrenic service user whose father was an accountant. He and the mother were both anxious and she was to be admitted to a psychiatric hospital in an acute anxiety state. His father said that he couldn't take her in alone and could I support him to do this? So I went to this large, expensive house and she was admitted. When the husband had driven me back he said would I like to go in for coffee? I didn't want to but I did. I went down this hallway and then into a room, then into another room. He shut the door behind me and I thought, 'He's going to murder me.' I was in an absolute panic but I stayed. I don't think that he had been violent but there was something about the way that he looked at me. I didn't think that he would sexually assault me but that he would murder me. He had these pale blue eyes... It was the most frightening experience that I've ever had. It was when I saw him after the door was shut that I had that feeling. It was kind of being alone with him... I didn't want to go in for coffee and don't know why. Having said 'yes' and gone in, I felt trapped. He wasn't big and powerful, it wasn't a physical thing, it was some emotional...chill that I experi-

enced. I remember his pale blue eyes, there was something inexplicable about it…it was associated with some kind of irrationality…

A number of participants in the research into fear described themselves as knowingly going against their intuition or 'better judgement' when deciding upon a course of action. This participant remembers her resistance to going in for coffee but also remembers how she 'over-ruled' this response. De Becker (1997) cautions against this, claiming that intuition should always be listened to. Although we may wrongly interpret messages from our intuition from time to time we should always listen to and respect it as, essentially, it functions as our protector, is always a response to *something* and always has our best interests at heart:

> Can you imagine an animal reacting to the gift of fear the way some people do, with annoyance and disdain instead of attention? No animal in the wild, suddenly overcome with fear, would spend any of its mental energy thinking, 'It's probably nothing'. (De Becker 1997, p.30)

Once again, 'nothing happened' in the real, external world and the participant emerged from the room to tell the tale. Others, choosing to ignore their intuition, may not have been so fortunate. The participant recalls her experience in visual, cinematic terms that might be filmed by Alfred Hitchcock, as she describes hallways and rooms of labyrinth qualities in hypnotic, surreal terms. As the man shuts the door behind her it is as if the actor Vincent Price featuring in an Edgar Allen Poe story rubs his hands with glee and chuckles ominously at the prospect of the evil he will go on to bring about. Again the participant denies her intuition: 'I was in an absolute panic but I stayed.'

Although the fears related by those who participated in the research into fear fell into a number of categories – fears of assault, death, losing control and separation – some people did not know what (specifically) they were frightened of. This participant was different. She was absolutely clear that she did not fear physical or sexual assault, but death. Like the participant just quoted she sets store on the communication from the 'pale blue eyes', as if they, particularly, speak the language of fear. It is of interest that the worker describes this as, 'the most frightening experience I've ever had' as, in a sense, there was no experience, other than in her imagination. It is also of interest that this particular worker recalled this incident so powerfully as she had worked as a qualified social worker for fifty years.

Despite all she had witnessed, heard and been involved with over these years, it was this memory of fear that had stayed with her and about which she wanted to talk in the research interview.

A male social worker working in Northern Ireland who also worked as a part-time fireman described the following experience:

> I was called out as a fireman to a person who had rowed with his wife. She had left the house and he had dowsed himself with inflammable liquid and threatened to set light to himself. I took off my fire brigade uniform and went in as a social worker and offered counselling. Once in the house I found he was taller than me. He was constantly pouring liquid on the floor and squirting it at me. He had maximum control. I was powerless. As soon as I came into the room he told me where to sit. He went next to the door and put me on the other side of the room. The police were trying to assemble a crash squad outside to disarm him. I tried to talk him round and reason with him but he was affected by alcohol and anger. He identified me as an authority figure who would punish him. He hadn't previously had a good response from social services. He was spraying me with barbecue fluid on my trousers, soaking the floor and the settee. I was scared shitless, the adrenaline was pumping. I thought, 'I'm going to be a victim…'. I said to him, 'I'm an innocent party here, if you're going to do it, don't take me with you.' The police said they were coming in and I jumped on the fella and struck the fuel from out of his hand. Four police then jumped on him. He was admitted to hospital under the Mental Health Act. After leaving the hospital where he was admitted I went home and experienced flashbacks. What would have happened if… These lasted for months and would occur in response to his name being mentioned or when I was driving past his place or if someone had set fire to a place or were lighting a barbecue.

As soon as the worker was in the room with the service user he felt powerless. He was smaller and, despite knowing that he should position himself by the door so as to ensure a quick exit if need be, found himself manipulated by the service user to the far side of the room and directed where to sit. This highlights a particular difficulty in relation to training workers to prepare proactively for frightening experiences and deal with these as they unfold. When people are afraid they are likely to forget what they know. Therefore, the most highly trained, knowledgeable and most skilful worker is likely to find his personal resources unavailable to him at the very time he needs them the most. This has implications for the type of training made available to workers and is further considered in Chapter Eight.

The worker's attempts to reason with the service user are of no avail. Workers find their usually-to-be-relied-upon ability to use words to get themselves out of danger often does not work in highly charged situations and this is another hallmark of fear-provoking experiences. The worker is held to blame for previously unsatisfactory relationships with the caring professions. The urge to defecate ('scared shitless') and adrenaline pumping were frequently reported reactions to fear. The worker sees the possibility of being moved from his rescuer role into that of victim and pleads with the service user that this is not right. Berne's (1975) description of the 'drama triangle' is relevant here. The drama triangle shows roles of victim, persecutor and rescuer at its three corners. Those in the caring professions see themselves in the 'rescuer' corner as they are essentially there to help others to achieve a less painful, healthier, more productive or satisfying life and to protect them from harm. However, people can move around from corner to corner of the triangle, sometimes extremely rapidly, and would-be 'rescuers' suddenly find themselves as victims. They may also find themselves feeling like persecutors too (see Chapter Five for examples of this). The drama triangle is a helpful model as it shows how the roles of 'helper' and 'helped' are not as different (i.e. as far away from one another) as they may seem to be at first sight.

The worker returns home and experiences flashbacks. Flashbacks are a feature of post-traumatic stress reaction and a common response to traumatic experiences. Organizations can help their staff by having measures in place that support those involved so that this type of (natural) reaction is less likely to deteriorate into a longer-term disorder (American Psychiatric Association 1994). A frequent question posed by this kind of experience is the extent to which people want or need to talk about what has happened and what has been imagined with their significant others (see Chapter Seven for a discussion of this matter).

Why did the worker knowingly put himself in such danger? Like the social worker quoted above, who thought she would be killed by the accountant, he may have questioned himself before going into the service user's house and yet decided not to be dissuaded from this course of action. He may have thought he would survive the danger (as, indeed, he did), 'could handle it' and would emerge having made a significant contribution with an impressive story to tell. May (1991) claims that many of those working in the caring professions are often motivated to do so by the 'hero myth'. The mythological hero engages in a quest whereby (usually) he exposes himself to peril and danger, vanquishes the enemy, and returns victorious. Jung (1978, p.61) writes that the myth:

> ...belongs to the world-wide and pre-Christ theme of the hero and rescuer who, although he has been devoured by a monster, appears again in a miraculous way, having overcome whatever monster it was that swallowed him... The hero figure is an archetype, which has existed since time immemorial.

Many working in health and social care today are inspired to do so because of a desire to fight a condition revealed as monstrous by personal history – disease, social injustice, violence, inequality, disability. Sometimes workers are unknowingly on a quest to face and vanquish fears they have partly recognized for years. In order to do so they have to put themselves in close proximity to the object of their fear so that they can fight it. In some cases the 'monster' may be the worker's fears.

A female social worker who was attacked by a service user she thought she knew well described her fear and its aftermath as follows:

> I was a senior social worker and had been working for quite a while with a woman in her early sixties who had an alcohol problem which she didn't acknowledge. She was also histrionic. I'd been helping her get re-housed. She had an old flat on the fourth floor. Outside there were concrete steps which circled up. There was a small balcony outside, about three feet high. I used to visit her regularly. On this particular day she'd phoned the secretary shouting, saying that she'd got problems. Entering her flat I found her not to be her usual self. She was very aroused. She was a powerful, big-built, stocky woman. She was shouting at me shaking her finger saying, 'You've got to sort this out immediately.' It was a rainy day and I had a plastic mac on. As usual, I was clutching my diary in one hand and a handbag in the other. We went to the kitchen to see what she was bothered about. She was very aroused. We bent down under the sink and she showed me the earth wire. I turned up, smiled, and said, 'That's perfectly all right' and she thought that I was laughing at her. She absolutely boiled over with rage and then got me up against the kitchen wall with her hands around my throat. The whole thing probably only took a matter of minutes although it felt very much longer. I've got all sorts of

visual memories of it, like a video with images that stay. That plastic mac I had on – I always felt it protected me. Looking back, it's totally irrational. I can't remember if her hands were around my skin or around the plastic – it may be that they were around the plastic and she couldn't get a grip. I felt a sense of protection at the time. I thought, 'I just don't know what to do.' I wasn't going to try and fight back because she was stronger than I was and absolutely raring to go. I can remember her stopping as if she thought, 'Oh, bugger this!' – a dismissive thing. I said, 'Let's not talk about it like this.' And we went into the sitting room and I said, 'Why don't you light a cigarette?' The moment her eyes were down and her hands were occupied I rushed out of the flat, absolutely terrified. I shook, I could hardly hold the diary. I was very shaky. I was surprised that my legs worked as well as they did, surprised that they did not give way… I do remember that I went home crying and it was as if I'd lost something – something about faith in human nature – something as silly as that. It perturbed me as I'd always thought that I'd had a good relationship with her. It's not an issue for me now, but if I press the button I can get the memory.

Again, the experience is recalled with a cinematic attention to detail as the storey of the building, the shape of the staircase and the height of the balcony are all remembered. The worker notices the service user to be 'not her usual self' but this does not stop her from proceeding with the visit alone. She remembers the strange sense of protection apparently afforded by the plastic mac. This resembles the 'comfortable feeling – that whatever happens you'll come to no harm' articulated by the nurse working with the man who saw everyone as being in the blues or the blacks and who is quoted above.

The worker recalls clutching her diary. As well as representing her professional role the diary includes both her past history and her future plans. This could be an indication of the extent to which the worker felt her identity, past and future, threatened by the assault. The fact that the worker smiled up at the service user is also important. Although intended to be reassuring and placatory, smiling also closely resembles snarling (Bowlby 1973) and may be perceived as a teeth-baring threat rather than a friendly, sympathetic communication to people who are highly aroused. The mention of video recalls the notions of performance and role discussed in Chapter Two. This experienced worker remembers herself as being at a loss about what to do – another example of even knowledgeable people forgetting what they know as a consequence of being afraid. She rules out the 'fight' option, is not quite 'frozen' as she accesses her capacity for thought sufficiently to encourage the service user to distract herself with a cigarette. This enables her to make her escape ('flight'). Workers are going to experience at least one of these three responses in response to fear-provoking stimuli and it is helpful for them to rehearse such situations to learn which of the three is most likely to affect them and how.

Another typical response to fear experienced by the worker is the shakiness and the feeling that her legs may not work (described by others as 'turning to jelly'). Fear typically shuts things down – physiologically, cognitively and emotionally – as people 'freeze'. The limbs do not work, the thoughts do not come and neither do the words as the mouth goes dry and the tongue may not function. Returning home, the worker mourned for something she felt she had lost – her faith in human nature. This is an indication of the potentially profound and far-reaching repercussions of an experience of fear. As a result of this experience the lone-visiting policies of this worker's team were entirely revised so as to promote safer working practices. Once again, the full impact of the fear is not felt so much in terms of what did happen but what might have happened. At its worst, the worker feared she might have been killed as a result of this visit to someone she thought she knew and could trust.

Recommendations for practice and training

- The dual and potentially mutually reinforcing fears of separation (being cut off from helpful others) and annihilation (self-destruction from within) should be acknowledged.

- Being a focus for service users' delusions can give rise to especially dangerous possibilities which should be subject to careful risk assessment.

- The influences of alcohol and substance misuse in compounding fears of service users which might then be projected on/into workers should be recognized.

- The tendency/likelihood of workers to disassociate in the face of threats should be allowed for and later addressed.

- The fact that workers might feel a strong and strange sense of protection (which may be real or illusory) while under threat should be acknowledged.

- Workers might have good reason(s) for fearing being killed while undertaking their duties and the gravity of these fears should be respected and addressed.

- The possibility of workers' 'assumptive worlds' being threatened by fear-provoking experiences when they feel forced into roles of victim and/or persecutor in relation to those they wanted to help should be recognized.

- The influence of the 'hero myth' on workers' responses in fear-provoking situations should be acknowledged.

- The fact that some workers might experience post-traumatic stress reaction, or even disorder, following some fear-provoking incidents should be addressed.

- The potential danger of smiling at service users in tense situations should be remembered.

Chapter 4

Working with Dangerous and Vulnerable Adults in Community Settings

Introduction

Throughout this chapter fears arising from work undertaken with service users who are thought to be vulnerable and/or potentially violent are considered. This group is distinguished from those who show violence as a consequence of suffering from a mental illness and who are discussed in Chapter Three. The influence of substance misuse on violent behaviour is illustrated and there is a particular focus on fears arising from work with older people. Fears of physical and sexual assault and death are considered. The importance of the 'secure base' and the relevance of the 'uncanny' are shown to be important. The use of humour following experiences of fear is discussed and the value of the concept of 'transference' illustrated.

Fears of violence

A duty social worker described seeing a service user to discuss a financial problem. The service user carried a bag and, looking down, the worker saw the handles of two ceremonial swords protruding from the end of the bag. She remembered reading some case notes about a man who had attacked his female partner with ceremonial swords and recalled:

> I was convinced he was going to pick this sword up and, with a ceremonial sweep, cut me in half. It was such a long knife. My blood ran cold. I turned to jelly, froze, as if a wave had gone over me, the shutters went down, a mask went over my face... I had not realized who I was talking to...women are taught to be afraid. Coming out of the room I made some jocular remark to the clerk that I had nearly had it in there.

In this account the worker again demonstrates the fear inspired by the imagination 'running riot' illustrated in previous chapters. There is a numbed certainty of being *doomed* or *done for*. While the worker clearly was not 'done for' as she survived the experience to tell its tale the fact that she believed, if only for a few moments, that she might die, is significant and clearly endured in her mind as having an emotional, if not a literal, reality. This feeling is the opposite to the belief that all shall be well and one will be safe, no matter how bad things look at a point in time, which is illustrated in Chapter Three.

In saying, 'My blood ran cold. I turned to jelly, froze' the worker articulates the sense of icy, creeping coldness often associated with the state of fear. The 'turning to jelly' conveys the sense of essential life blood seeping away, as Coleridge [1802] (1987) puts it, 'Fear at my heart, as at a cup, My life-blood seemed to sip!' The worker also demonstrates how vividly her imagination sets to work, even when recalling her experience, as she employs metaphors of freezing, jelly, a wave, shutters and a mask within a few words. She describes the fears of one essentially ill informed who did not know what they were doing, or just *who* they were seeing. This is a 'near-miss' (lucky escape) experience similar to that experienced by people who were innocently talking to a stranger they later discovered to be a murderer. She goes on to reflect upon the wider and further-reaching implications of violence by men against women which cause women to learn that they should be afraid (see Herman 2001).

Coming out of the interview room the worker recalls seeing a clerk. Administrative and reception staff feature repeatedly and importantly in workers' accounts of fear, probably because they are the identifiable patrollers and keepers of the office (secure) base that workers go out from and return to (Bowlby 1988). Administrative and reception staff are frequently confided in and will often have considerable knowledge of where a worker is going, who they are visiting, how they get on with them, what they think of them and when they are expecting to return. The worker refers to making 'some jocular remark' to the clerk; the use of humour by those in extremely dangerous and threatening situations is well known and documented (Berne 1975; Kuhlman 1988; Sullivan 2000). Humour and jokes essentially depend upon seeing something from a different perspective (Freud 1961). Because of this, if humour is used well, in appropriate ways, and at the right time, it can be one of the most helpful responses to traumatic situations. Used insensitively, in the wrong way, at the wrong time, failed attempts at humour can be remembered for years to come as worsening rather than healing a trauma.

One example of an attempt at humour intended to help but falling far short of its mark was given by a social worker who had just returned to his office from hearing the tragic news that a young mother he worked with had jumped from a high building with her baby in her arms, killing them both. He recalled his manager telling him, 'You should have caught the baby.' While this can be appreciated as an attempt to see a situation from a different point of view and to convey to the worker that he could not have prevented the tragedy the worker's memory of the comment was that it was inappropriate and insensitive.

Another example of a fear of violence was shared by a female worker when working as a housing officer:

> As a housing officer it was part of my job to carry out evictions of people who were squatting. I went into one of our short life properties and saw that I was surrounded by eight men all with things in their hands they could have beaten me to a pulp with. I went through the door and they were up on the first floor. It was not until I got into the room and stood in the centre that I realized there were eight of them. One had what looked like a chopper, and another an iron bar. I said, 'OK – you can beat me to a pulp but you're still going to have to leave.' They were looking at each other, not quite sure of what they were going to do. I was maintaining eye contact with one person and telling him when I said it. I then looked at the others, they looked at each other to see if anyone was going to make the first move and it was apparent that no one was going to take the lead… Getting back to the office I was laughing, joking – saying silly things like, 'I nearly had my head chopped off, ho, ho, ho…' They weren't sure of how serious it was because of the way that I was talking about it… I felt it more a couple of days afterwards when I was sat at

home and had put the boys to bed. I thought, 'That was a bit dangerous really, I've got two kids…that was dangerous' [laughs] – I didn't dwell on it really.

Again a woman is threatened with violence from men. Her response is to take charge in a way that seems to have reduced or removed the threat. The suddenness with which fear-provoking incidents can unexpectedly emerge from the shadows when one is engaged in one's routine work is apparent. Again the attempted use of humour can be seen. In this case the use of humour causes those hearing of the incident some difficulty in ascertaining how serious it actually was. This seems more like a 'manic defence' against a threat than a cathartic use of humour. The worker shows how responses to fear might only become apparent with the passing of time. Following her initial denial of the seriousness of the threat, having put her children to bed (a time evocative of particular vulnerability) she appraises the event more thoughtfully and realistically. Interestingly, she attempts to use humour again, by laughing when she recalls the experience.

Sometimes the fear experienced may relate primarily to a sexual rather than a physical threat as the next two accounts, both recalled by female counsellors, show:

I saw this man who said things where nothing tied up. I judged him to be about 65. He had straggly long grey hair, an unpleasant appearance. He was a stereotype of a 'dirty old man'. He said he was 49 and that didn't tie up. He talked of sexual experiences with women in their twenties and of the tremendous anger that he had towards them. He was so 'sick-making' talking about sex and violence – being almost voyeuristic, he was trying to shock. Whenever he came into contact with a woman it was all *vibrant* and *wonderful*. He said odd things like, 'I was originally angry against women who let me down but since doing line dancing I have got rid of these feelings.' I only saw him once and for two or three weeks after the time I saw him I was afraid that he might be in the car park, waiting for me.

It was a dark and wintry night, the wind was howling, and I had gone to a block of flats to see a man for our first meeting. The door was suddenly pulled open and he was a man of about four feet and six inches tall and very strange looking. He bolted the door with a number of bolts and I felt trapped. He talked about sex and it was clear that he had difficulties forming relationships with women who wondered whether or not he could perform. He looked at my wedding ring and I felt uncomfortable… I feared he may sexually assault me.

In both of these accounts women fear sexual assault from men which does not materialize but which seems to be knowingly introduced by both men as being a distinct possibility. The man in the first account talked of a sexual relation, 'whenever he came into contact with a woman'. It would not have escaped the counsellor's notice that she was a woman who had come into contact with him. Despite the counsellor only seeing him once, he played (preyed?) on her mind for several weeks as she feared he might be waiting for her by her car, once she was away from the protection of the secure base.

In the second account the experience is recalled with the cinematic attention to detail apparent in previous accounts. The stage and scene are set as the man bolts the woman into his territory. 'Nothing happened' to the counsellor in the real, external world but, once again, the 'shaping spirit' of imagination can be seen at work. Both accounts have a surreal, almost dream-like, quality to them bringing to mind Freud's (1955c) concept of the 'uncanny' (also translated as 'unhomely') which comprises both recognized and unrecognized aspects of fear, 'a peculiar commingling of the familiar and unfamiliar' (Royle 2003, p.1). Feeling and thinking that one both recognizes and, simultaneously, does not recognize a source of fear is confusing and disorientating in the extreme. One notices something but 'nothing adds up', like in a dream.

The importance of receptionists and administrative workers to health and social care workers in providing and patrolling a secure base has been mentioned previously. Sometimes, however, it is the receptionists and reception areas that are under threat:

A guy stormed through Reception with a fencing pole, smashing windows, and broke down the door between Reception and our area. We were all ushered out pretty quickly and it was pretty traumatic. He had a lot of grievances and was aiming for a particular social worker who wasn't there at the time.

On one occasion we were in our office and there was a sliding window on Reception which was left open almost all the time and a female client high on drink, and possibly drugs, had a pipe cleaning knife and was making demands. Another administrative worker kind of laughed and she jumped through the window and grabbed him and was holding the knife to his face and neck… He only went 'Huh huh' and that was it, that was all it took, and she was through the window.

As they take decisions which might prove unpopular concerning crucial aspects of people's lives, such as the right to be free, and the right to bring up children in the manner one thinks best, social workers will provide a focus for the rage and discontent of dissatisfied service users. Although the police can be called as a matter of urgency to such extreme incidents, as they were in the two instances quoted above, delays in their response can be crucial. One fears for what might have happened to the social worker being sought in the first instance were she at her desk. The second example shows how a relatively small contribution to a situation can make a profound difference to its outcome, particularly when highly aroused and dis-inhibited people are involved. The perceived similarities between a smile and a snarl are discussed in Chapter Three and the fear of being laughed at (ridiculed) is particularly hard to bear. The thought that one has been humiliated is therefore likely to act as a catalyst for those seeking an outlet for pent-up frustration and rage. The second quotation refers to a client thought to be under the influence of alcohol and/or drugs. The fears of dis-inhibition resulting from substance misuse featured many times in workers' accounts of their fears and are now considered.

Alcohol and substance misuse

A counsellor recalled visiting a client to find:

She had been drinking cider throughout most of the evening and told me that she had hit a policewoman in the past and I thought, 'Uh-oh, this lady could be vicious.' She drank quite a lot. You worry that people are going to change. I suppose I feared would she have lashed out or something? Would she have got aggressive – she'd been drinking…she might have lashed out… I might have said something…

The counsellor's concern that she 'might have said something' that antago-nized the client serves as a useful cautionary thought as the case of the young woman with the pipe cleaning knife, quoted above, shows. In this instance the administrative worker might not have been sufficiently cautious when communicating to anticipate how this communication might be perceived by the client. The counsellor was not assaulted on this occasion but was alive to the possibility that when the client was referring to a previous instance of hitting a policewoman she might have been alerting the counsellor to her potential for violence against women 'authority figures', possibly including the counsellor. It is helpful for workers in health and social care settings to be aware of this capacity of people to 'transfer' experiences from the past into the present by way of 'transference' (Jacobs 1988; Storr 1992) as clients may temporarily 'see' workers as (representing) significant others against whom they carry unexpressed grievances. Workers may therefore be attacked, not necessarily because of who *they* are or what *they* have done (or not done) but because of who they remind the client of. A male community mental health nurse described being assaulted while seeing a man who became angry with him:

> A man I saw has a habit of doing pretty well and then getting really drunk. He was talking of his physical prowess and how strong he is. To demonstrate this he picked me up and said something he has done, or that he would feel like doing, is to throw a person out of the window. He comes to see a therapist but he has the power in physical strength, 'You can be the therapist, so what? I can throw you out of the window. To hell with your therapy.' So no matter how you do your therapy in this kind of context it's irrelevant.

Annoyed and irritated at the power imbalance he perceives the service user sets about rectifying this. It is difficult to see his reaction as resulting only from his contact with the nurse on the occasion they met. It is more instructive to think about this within the wider context of his past relationships which he might have been transferring on to the nurse. Confrontations with service users under the influence of alcohol and/or who have abused substances can be profoundly disconcerting as the following account from a male social worker illustrates:

> I was in a multi-storey block of flats visiting a woman with an alcohol problem. I was trying to deal with her aggression and intoxication. She punched me and I went down. I knew that I should use her first name and try to calm things down. There were local hoods and glue-sniffers in the flat who all had chips on their shoulders and saw me as part of 'the system'. She was saying to them that this was their chance to get their own back. There must have been about eight or ten of them by several

doors. They were half spaced out and treating it as entertainment. I was thinking that I needed to get back. I got into the lift and it stopped. The doors opened and she was there. I tried to get down the stairs and she came down the stairs. I was trying to rap doors to get into other people's flats to get help. She was trying to get into the lift with me. I was holding on to my diary and knew that if those lift doors closed with her inside them then I would have to do something. I would have to react. It's her or me, and it's going to be me, who comes out... I would have thought 'To hell with the job – this is jungle stuff – I'm going to come out.' There would only have been the 'fight' option left. The fear extends and projects onto everything. On the way out I passed two girls who I had seen when trying to get out of the building earlier. My eyes must have been like saucers. I don't remember the drive back to the office at all. At its most extreme it was a fear of death, of non-existence, of having to survive. I fled like a rabbit. It was so primal, so gut. I haven't looked at the police statement I made at the time. You don't want to go back. There was a loss of control. It was like a cheap video. Once out of the building I didn't know which end of me was up. It was overwhelming, incapacitating, it affects your brain. There's still gaps. I sat down with the police to make a statement but I couldn't remember. There was blood over my shirt, skin off my knuckles. Fear cripples. I remember holding on to my diary – my professional role – but by the third time I'd lost it...

This graphic account illustrates many significant aspects of fear-provoking experiences. Like the housing officer quoted above the worker fears being turned on by an angry group although in this instance at least some of the group appeared to be under the influence of substances they had abused. This could be in the worker's favour, if the substance abuse resulted in the group being less motivated or able to attack, or against him, if the substances lowered the group's inhibitions and social controls against committing acts of violence and therefore made the possibility of attack more likely. Either way, a dis-inhibited group is likely to follow a 'horde' mentality, as, when part of a group, individuals are likely to restrain themselves less readily and less easily than they would do if alone:

...the fact that individuals have been transformed into a group puts them in possession of a sort of collective mind which makes them feel, think, and act in a manner quite different from that in which each individual of them would feel, think and act were he in a state of isolation...the individual forming part of a group acquires a sentiment of invincible power which allows him to yield to instincts which, had he been alone, he would perforce have kept under restraint...a group being anonymous and in consequence irresponsible, the sentiment of responsibility which always controls individuals disappears entirely. (Freud 1955b, pp.73–4)

The influence of the group is rightly to be feared. In both this instance and that recalled by the housing officer it seemed that no one individual was prepared to take the initiative to unite the group and lead it in action. Had a leader been forthcoming, the outcome might have been considerably worse in both cases.

The theme of playing a role (Berne 1975) is again apparent in this account as the worker recalls being treated as entertainment on a cheap video. The worker's comment, 'I was thinking that I needed to get back' is an interesting one. On one level he seems to be articulating his awareness of the need to return to his office (secure) base. Simultaneously, at a deeper level he might be acknowledging a desire to 'get back' to his pre-traumatized self. Later in his account he states, 'You don't want to go back' i.e. remember or get back in touch with the fear-provoking experience, thereby illustrating the ambivalence with which most people think of their fears (see Chapter One). Like a character in a Stephen King novel the woman appears when any door opens, blocking his exit. His attempts to connect with others who might help fail and his separation anxiety (Bowlby 1973) is at its height as people in nearby flats do not respond to his assistance-seeking knocks.

Like the mental health worker held by the throat by the service user quoted in Chapter Three the worker recalls holding on to his diary which contains his past and intended future – a summary of his identity. His very identity appears to be under threat as he envisages harming, even killing the person he was visiting to help a few minutes previously (see discussion of the 'drama triangle' in Chapter Three). 'This is jungle stuff' articulates the eat-or-be-eaten primitive aspects of survival he believes to be at stake as he gives words to his fears of annihilation, '...a fear of death, of non-existence, of having to survive'. His observing self describes his traumatized self as he imagines how others must have seen him: 'My eyes must have been like saucers.' The extract conveys how profoundly experiences of fear, even if only lasting a few minutes, can disorientate those affected: 'The fear extends and projects onto everything...I didn't know which end of me was up. It was overwhelming, incapacitating, it affects your brain... Fear cripples.'

Working with people who have abused alcohol and/or other substances can increase the possibility of being at the receiving end of dis-inhibited and therefore more aggressive behaviours which cause workers to fear for their safety, and, on occasions, even for their lives. While particular risks might be posed by these service users none can be guaranteed as risk-free. Working with older people can be dangerous too.

Older people

When accompanying an older person for what should have been a routine hospital appointment one worker told of how the service user's demeanour abruptly changed without warning or apparent reason: 'She knocked my glasses off and clawed at my face and eyes.' For another worker it was not the fear of assault that she remembered but the horrific aftermath of visiting a female service user whose husband had just died from a violent haemorrhage and whose body was still in the room when she visited. She found her imagination 'running riot' as she put herself in the place of the service user, wondering how she would manage if it were her husband who had died.

A home carer recalled:

> I was visiting this place that was very remote, dark and spooky, there was a river running by the back. It was so dark that I could not see where I had parked the car and I had forgotten my torch. Suddenly a man grabbed hold of my arm and asked if he could have a lift to the next village. I said 'No' but he said, 'I've been watching you and know that you see others in the village.' I was afraid of what might happen.

This account demonstrates how it is not always the service user who is the source of fear and that workers take risks when getting to and from their places of work. Visits to frail and vulnerable adults out of normal office hours have increased over recent years as people are increasingly being supported to stay in their own homes. Visiting these people alone in remote places, however, is becoming increasingly rare as working alongside a colleague as a matter of course has become increasingly common.

The carer's fear encapsulates Freud's (1959) major components of a frightening experience – to be alone, in the dark, then joined by a stranger who bodes no good. Again, the experience is recalled with a cinematic eye for detail, vividly conjuring up an evocative sense of place and setting. The car is described as if a secure base, a would-be safe place for the carer to return to, although in this instance it is invisible in the darkness. The sudden and unexpected appearance of a stranger who claimed to have been watching the carer is like something from a horror novel and, again, the influence of the disorientating 'uncanny' is apparent. The carer made her escape safely and without incident but the impact of the experience was such that she did not continue visiting service users at night.

While visiting in pairs affords workers some safety and protection even this is no absolute guarantee of safety as the following experience of two home carers visiting a terminally ill service user together illustrates:

> Early one evening we were visiting a lady who was dying when this man came towards us walking down the road. I thought, 'That man's drunk' and tried to avoid eye contact (I was married to a violent alcoholic so I knew the signs). He punched one of us in the face and grabbed the back of the hair of another and kept smacking her head against the wall. We were afraid of what could have happened. He could have raped us. If he had a knife he could have killed us.

Again, the carers experience fear while on their way to work. Even though one carer spotted the 'warning signs' of the man's behaviour this did not protect her, or keep her colleague safe. The attack was unprovoked and began and ended without apparent reason or trigger. The carer's recollection demonstrates how people do not necessarily know what they are frightened of. The fears in this incident included fears of physical assault, rape, or even death. Typically, however, it was not what was happening that was feared as much as what might yet be to happen. Workers coped with extremely difficult and worrying attacks in the present and almost appeared to take these 'as read', comparatively they took them in their stride. What seemed worse and more to be feared was the uncertainty of what might be just around the corner that they could not know in the present moment. Because fear is essentially anticipatory and entails looking forward, attempting to predict the future, fears can never be conclusively disproved or denied. No one can state with certainty that the feared-for event will not come to pass.

Home carers may encounter violent relatives while caring for service users:

> I was speaking to an old lady when her son came at me, shouting verbal abuse and poking his finger at my throat. He went berserk and was very intimidating. Even the old lady was frightened and tried to tell him that it was all right but he didn't take any notice. I said, 'I'm leaving' and as I went to leave he grabbed my arm. I was very frightened. I managed to pull away and I ran out. I ran to another lady (a neighbour) who could see I was upset and she gave me a cup of tea. Then I called my husband and he came to take me home.

Sometimes carers will find themselves caught up in complex relationships between those caring and cared for. Family members might have feelings of anger and resentment against those caring for their relative as well as gratitude. Carers might experience displaced abusive behaviours, normally directed towards the family member they are caring for.

This carer called on her husband for help and this illustrates another dilemma faced by those affected by fear-provoking incidents encountered at work – how much to share them with significant others at home. In this instance the carer told her husband of what had happened quickly but others might decide not to share such experiences for fear of a well-intended but unwelcome over-reaction from their partner. One carer said, 'My husband said, "That's outrageous" and wanted to go round and sort the person out.' Another reported, 'On hearing what had happened to me my husband went upstairs and started pulling the bathroom wallpaper off, and, he wasn't decorating!' While people wanted to be supported by significant others following fear-provoking experiences, and part of this support was not having the impact of their experience under-represented, they did not want their experiences misrepresented by way of over-reaction. Several female workers reported their male partners wanted to 'sort things out' or had simplistic solutions to multi-faceted situations such as, 'Well, don't go there any more then.' They did not find these responses helpful as they preferred first to discuss and explore the complexities of situations without being rushed too quickly into analysis and solution.

Recommendations for practice and training

- The use of humour as both potentially extremely helpful and unhelpful responses to fear-provoking incidents should be recognized. Humour should therefore be used with caution.

- Physiological changes in workers facing fears such as feeling their blood run cold and limbs turn to jelly should be accepted as the norm and anticipated.

- The importance and potential vulnerability of administrative/reception staff who provide immediate and 'front-line' contact with distressed service users and workers should be valued and thought about.

- The multiple, changing and evolving nature of workers' responses to traumatic experiences over time should be acknowledged and allowed for.

- The concept of 'transference' whereby fears might be transferred onto/into workers who remind service users of past experiences should be recognized.

- Ways in which perceived power imbalances might frustrate service users and provoke them to violence should be acknowledged.

- Particular threats posed to workers by anti-establishment angry groups should be anticipated.

- Again, workers' ambivalence in relation to their fears should be appreciated. They might experience a desire to 'get back' to a secure base and pre-traumatized mental state along with a simultaneous reluctance to 'get back' to traumatic memories by way of recalling them.

- Primitive needs to survive might be awakened in workers under threat and the disturbing force of these needs should be recognized.

- The importance of the car as a secure base in and of itself or as a transitional object that conveys workers to the perceived safety of a secure base should be acknowledged.

- The fact that family members of service users (about whom little or nothing might be known) may pose a greater threat to workers than the service users themselves should be appreciated.

- It should be remembered that fear is a complex and multi-faceted emotion. Angry, simplistic responses to it are not helpful, however well-intentioned.

Chapter 5

Residential and Institutional Settings

Introduction

This chapter begins with examples of residential workers fearing violence and/or death. The role of 'the gothic' in the recall of frightening incidents is apparent. The examples show how workers can dissociate, as a professional care-taking self seems to step in and take over from the threatened, traumatized self. When extremely frightened, people can forget to apply the safe practices they have learned as previous knowledge and skills desert them. Fear-provoking experiences come suddenly and unexpectedly; sense of time is distorted. People feel a need to 'get back' to a secure base; both externally, to an office, and internally, to connect with the pre-traumatized self. Colleagues are shown to be of crucial importance in helping workers to deal with incidents appropriately. Fears of sexual assault and the accompanying feelings of shame and embarrassment are illustrated as are workers' 'fight' responses to fear. In extreme instances workers have wanted to harm, or even kill, the young people in their care, such has been the force of the desire to retaliate when threatened.

Fears of violence and death

Balloch, Pahl and McLean (1998) have shown that, of all social care workers, residential workers are the most likely to be exposed to violence and threats of violence. Residential workers in children's homes are particularly affected. One worker recalls an occasion when in sole charge of a residential unit for young people:

I had got involved in an altercation concerning a client not getting out of bed. I dealt with the matter through appropriate channels. Some evenings later I was on night duty. The place was an old, large, rambling house and I was the only person on duty, all the other staff had gone home. All of the clients were supposed to be in bed and I was coming along a dimly lit hallway and was met by three of my clients aged between 14 and 18, dressed in anoraks with hoods up. One guy had a knife. They advised me that they didn't like the way that I had handled this situation with regard to one of their peers and that they were going to carve me up. They were stood there with knives. I did a double take when I saw the knife. In my military career previously I had been a physical training instructor and taught unarmed combat so being faced with knives was not an unusual scenario but in this totally different context I had no skills. I turned to go up the stairs and was waiting for this knife to go into my back. I just kept walking, and the fear… I went up the stairs on 'auto' but felt a kind of giddy blacking out fear – a white haze, having gone up the stairs, seeing the wall coming and going. People have said to me since that had the knife gone in I would not have felt it because of this giddy feeling. I can't really recall what happened but nothing happened and then I felt immediately that I wanted to share what had happened but there wasn't anyone around.

This account comprises many aspects of fear related by participants in the research. The worker believes he has dealt with something only to discover that he has not. Being alone on night duty in a large, rambling, dimly lit house gives the memory a gothic quality (Botting 1996). At bedtime, when the clients should have been safely and quietly asleep or preparing for sleep a threat emerges from the shadows. A small group in hoods perpetuates the gothic atmosphere. Threats were made but, perhaps because no one took the initiative and led the group (see Chapter Four), not fulfilled. The worker denies what he sees ('I did a double take') and illustrates how fear can banish people's previously acquired knowledge and skills, rendering them inaccessible at times of need. This man was an expert in unarmed combat and had taught it to others. If anyone was well qualified to deal with this particular threat he was, but despite this, he found himself unable to access his own resources. If workers are to be deserted by their knowledge and skills at times of need how can they be effectively trained to function in spite of the paralysis that is a consequence of their fears?

The worker describes a dissociation (Sinason 2002) whereby a professional care-taker self takes over from his traumatized self, which felt almost too giddy to stand, leading him up the stairs 'on auto'. Extremes of black and white converge as he recalls a blacking out fear along with a white haze. The fear is such that it alters his perception of stationary buildings as the wall appears to 'come and go' with his giddiness. Once again, 'nothing happens' in the external world but a great deal has taken place inside his head. The worker articulates this confusion about whether or not anything has 'happened' when he says, 'I can't really recall what happened but nothing happened and then I felt immediately that I wanted to share what had happened.' Although described many years after it took place, the confusion brought about by fear along with the uncertainty as to what, if anything, had actually happened is economically conveyed.

Two female residential workers described occasions when 'nothing happened' in the external world but which caused them to fear for their lives:

> We had restrained a kid of ten who always used to calm down and have tears afterwards. The other staff had gone downstairs and everyone had assumed that he had calmed down. He then put his fingers in an electric socket and said, 'If I go, then I'm taking you with me.' He then went into a deeper woe about his family and there was this can of worms in front of me. I could hear the other staff laughing downstairs. The fear initially was, 'I'm going to die.' This was relatively short lived and was taken over by the fear that I didn't have the capability to help this boy with what was coming out of his mouth.

> We had a young person who had stolen knives from a cabinet. I was supposed to go and find some knives with him and so the two of us went looking for them in some woods next to the Unit about 7.00pm on a summer's evening. We couldn't find them. He had just helped to pull me out of a dip when he suddenly pulled a bread knife on me and held it across the back of my neck. He said, 'This is what you've always wanted.' I looked up at the trees and thought, 'I'm going to die.' He was trying to strangle me and get me to the ground to do whatever he wanted. The fear was of how vulnerable I felt. I started crying and he threw the knife away... I knew I had to get back to the Unit to feel safe. I don't know where I got the strength from. I was on automatic pilot. I know we're told not to show emotion but the tears kind of snapped him out of it. For

> many years after, this came back to me. If a 13-year-old could do this what could a man do? I went home and couldn't stop shaking and crying. I had a week off but there weren't any services offered to me and I felt angry with the department. They don't take attacks on staff generally on board.

Once again, apparently safe, calm and dealt-with situations suddenly transform into something dangerous, even life-threatening. Workers recall being separated from attachment figures who might help. In the first example the sound of laughter from a distant room highlights this separation in a way which seems to mock the worker left alone. The second worker feels 'doomed' (see Chapter Four) as, for a time, her death seems possible or likely. Like the male worker quoted above, this worker also recalls a professional self stepping in and taking over from her traumatized self leaving her needing only to relinquish control to her 'automatic pilot'. While the advice generally given to people in fearful situations is not to show their emotions (De Becker 1997) this worker's experience shows that no single response can be appropriate for all occasions. In this instance it seems that it was by showing emotion that the worker ensured her safe escape. Although 'nothing happened' the impact of the experience remained with her for years and was powerfully apparent in her recollection of it.

In the examples given so far the workers concerned suffered no actual harm, despite their fears. On other occasions, however, workers were physically harmed:

> I was assaulted by a young person who had his teeth in my hand and was holding on. My hand was going numb and he crushed my nerve so I could not feel. I had a fear of what he had done, a fear of letting him go and a fear of how the damage may affect me in the future. When I returned to the unit after two days off I had a fear that it would happen again. I feared that the damage may be permanent. It was six months before I knew that the damage was not permanent.

This worker's account shows the repercussions that can follow an incident lasting only a few seconds. She describes fear of the past, present and future combined as she wonders what the young person has done, was doing and might yet do. She returns to work fearing that the incident might be repeated. At least this worker was able to return to work. The aftermath of some assaults on residential workers has been such that they have been signed off work with Post Traumatic Stress Disorder and have been unable to resume their work at all (Smith 1999).

A deputy head of a rehabilitation unit for adults with a learning disability recalled the impact of an unexpected assault and its immediate aftermath:

> I knocked on a client's door and heard a verbal acknowledgement to go in. He was washing himself. He smiled, then charged at me, punching me in the face. He pushed me back out of the room and then slammed the door in my face. The fear was of trying to make contact with the individual again. He was very unpredictable. The assault was in contrast to the smile and the wave with which he had greeted me. I was the only staff member on duty. The person taking over from me was not due for another hour and a quarter. I didn't know what had instigated the attack and feared that he would do it again. There was a quiver in my voice, my speech became more rapid and my hands were shaking. An hour and a quarter seemed like a lifetime. I tried to get control of myself and my feelings. I couldn't let him know I was afraid so I went back to see him but as I was standing outside his door I saw the handle of the door turn and ran back downstairs. If I would have been able to knock on the door I would have felt in control but on seeing the door handle turn I felt the control go and fear overcame me again. I could have phoned the colleague due to come in but to do so would have been to acknowledge that I had lost control. I thought of the safety of other residents and was getting them away from the kitchen and the knives... I kept hoping and praying that the staff member due to take over from me would come around the corner. When she did come in I immediately off-loaded myself. I unleashed myself at her. She was a junior member of staff as well... I could have upended that woman.

This worker conveys her struggle to regain and retain her composure and balance in the aftermath of a fearful experience. Time is distorted as an hour and quarter seems like a lifetime. The worker struggles with the desire to cope unaided and the desire to ask for help. This is compounded by the fact that she is the senior member of staff and reluctant to expose her vulnerability to a junior colleague. The worker is aware of shaking and of not speaking as confidently as she usually would. Frightened people will sometimes find themselves unable to speak at all as their mouth dries up and their tongue does not respond to attempts to move it around. Just as useful skills were unavailable to the male worker threatened by the young people with knives appropriate words were unavailable to this worker. She finds herself 'catastrophizing' as she imagines the resident seeking out knives to harm others. When the unsuspecting colleague does arrive the worker's resolve to stay strong gives way like a dam bursting as she 'unleashes' herself with a force she later regrets. If not allowed appropriate outlets fears can gain momentum and find expression with inappropriate force at unsuitable times.

Sometimes threats of violence were made when young people had abused alcohol or other substances and so were more dis-inhibited than usual:

> One young person sprayed hairspray at us and lit the vapour so it was like he had a flame thrower. The only response was to flee. He was so out of his head that you couldn't reason with him. I went into the office and called the police who arrived in about twenty seconds. The police took the hairspray/torch away from him which relieved the fear.

Some staff were confronted with riots:

> Two young people were throwing stones from the roof, aiming at hitting the staff. There was a lot of noise and abuse. I feared it would get worse and I feared for my safety. I also feared that these young black guys would get in more trouble with the law (they were already in enough trouble) and there would be further criminal instances added to their record.

Some staff were taken hostage:

> Four of us were taken hostage in the living room for two hours by two young people. I feared that it might get more aggressive, more violent, and that someone might get seriously hurt. I thought that my ribs would be broken if I was rammed in the corner of the wall again. One young person had her hands around a staff member's throat and squeezed. We couldn't get to a phone. We were in the living room for two hours but it felt like an age. I felt near to tears. I was physically shaking. Someone had to put gum between their teeth to stop the noise they were making. I wondered how we would gain control. They were later charged with actual bodily harm, criminal damage and threats to kill. The worker who was threatened believed that they would kill her.

Once again, an unsuspecting worker is suddenly forced to consider the possibility that she might be killed. Fears of being assaulted, losing control and being killed are combined in this account. On other occasions fears might be more specific such as the fear of sexual assault which is now related.

Fear of sexual assault

A female residential social worker recalled:

> There were about four boys in a bedroom playing with a computer and I'd had some trouble with a 13-year-old who was being a bit sexual. He was physical, wanting affection, wanting a hug. There were three staff on and the other two were in the kitchen. I walked into the bedroom just to check on the boys and he grabbed me as if to hug me but he grabbed my bum and my boob and pushed me towards the bed saying, 'Come on, come on…' The others were laughing and cajoling him, 'Go on, go on…' They could be quite sexual at times. I didn't think that he would try to rape me. He might get me on the bed so that he could squash me and try to pull off my bra. I felt very vulnerable. The other boys probably wouldn't have helped me unless it turned into something that was very serious. It turned out that he may have sexually abused his sister when he was younger.

This account highlights the difficulties that can be experienced by those working and living in close proximity to children whose life experiences to date do not equip them to establish and maintain appropriate physical and sexual boundaries. Cairns (1999) describes the impact for carers looking after young children who, when asked for a goodnight kiss, attempt to kiss an adult with an open mouth. If the primary form of most communications in a child's experience has been sexual, how can they learn when this is not appropriate? Residential workers caring for children who have been abused will inevitably become caught up in this maelstrom. They cannot avoid powerful and only partly recognizable transference and countertransference feelings which are an intrinsic feature of these dynamics (see Chapter Four). How others subsequently respond to these experiences will shape and influence the extent of their impact. The worker continues:

> The social worker said I should think of telling the police and making a complaint. I spoke to the young person about this and said that I had

filled in a Health and Safety form and had thought about going to the police but wasn't going to. He said, 'I was only joking. You can't take a joke, you silly old cow.' He said to the others, 'Don't talk to her, she'll go to the police even though she's coming on strong to you.'

The female victim of assault is made out to be the perpetrator by the young person who blames her and attempts to turn his peers against the worker. The way in which the wider staff group recognize and respond to the worker's needs for affirmation and support is therefore vital. This is particularly important as feelings of embarrassment and shame are near, yet distinct, neighbours of fear:

> ...shame is the affect of indignity, of defeat, of transgression, and of alienation. Though terror speaks to life and death and distress makes the world a vale of tears, yet shame strikes deepest into the heart of (wo)man. (Sedgwick and Frank 1995, p.133)

For Erikson [1951] (1977) shame is the second of eight life stages necessary for all individuals to negotiate. Even when individuals are successful in dealing with it in infancy, like all life stages, it requires frequent reconsideration at later times in life. Shame often relates to bodily or sexual functioning:

> Shame is an emotion insufficiently studied, because in our civilization it is so early and easily absorbed by guilt. Shame supposes that one is completely exposed and conscious of being looked at: in one word, self-conscious. One is visible and not ready to be visible; which is why we dream of shame as a situation in which we are stared at in a condition of incomplete dress, in night attire, 'with one's pants down'. Shame is early expressed in an impulse to bury one's face, or to sink, right then and there, into the ground. (Erikson [1951] 1977, p.227)

Shame and fear are so closely associated as the shame of being exposed (made too visible) is closely linked with the fear of what the consequences of this might be. Having some understanding of the frequent and extreme threats made to residential workers and the assaults they suffer, it is not surprising that they might, at times, feel like retaliating. The desire to hit out as a way of defending oneself is often experienced as an instinctive protective mechanism. It can show people aspects of themselves that they find it difficult to integrate into their self-image and this might cause them concern at a later date. Consideration of this desire entails the recognition of another near neighbour of fear: anger.

Fears of desires for retaliation

The 'drama triangle' (Berne 1975) was introduced in Chapter Three. This model suggests that people initially occupy a particular corner of the triangle: in roles of victim, persecutor or rescuer. Those working in health and social care are likely to see themselves primarily as rescuers. If threatened or assaulted, however, they might become potential or actual victims. In their desire to protect and defend themselves or others they can become persecutors. Sometimes, despite being angry, workers retained sufficient insight into their behaviours to realize the potential danger of what they were doing, or might have gone on to do, and to stop it:

> A young person was trying to spit in a female staff member's face and punch her. I pinned him down on the floor and thought, 'You've lost it, you're on the floor' and he was still wanting to hit her. I just walked off because I really wanted to punch him in the face.

> There was this young person who was trying to dominate and disrupt everything. Things were building up and he turned off the music that we had on and threw the tape onto the floor. I grabbed him and decked him, got him around the throat and said, 'If you don't stop it I'll lose my job because of you.'

Workers feared that young people knew the power they held in making a complaint. In most establishments if a young person made a complaint against a worker that worker would be suspended and denied contact with colleagues while the complaint was investigated. Although there are valid reasons for this course of action in terms of employment legislation, from the worker's point of view complaints can weaken and sever links with the very group they want to belong to. Extreme separation anxiety can consequently be activated. The worker experiences different fears on various levels at the same time. They fear an assault and its potential consequences; simultaneously they fear that they will not be supported if they protect themselves:

> One evening a young person refused to leave the room of another resident. I wanted to show the young person that there were rules and

that we wanted him to abide by them. I talked myself into a corner though and didn't allow myself any way out. I picked him up in a fireman's lift and moved him. He'd been threatening me and had been charged with GBH for smashing a bottle over someone's head. He threw a shoe at a female staff member's head and picked up a fire extinguisher and threw it at my head. He had no care or regard for other people's lives. Staff have been fearful about what they can't do. A staff member has been suspended for doing their job. You have to defend yourself and prove your innocence. You think that you're guilty until proved innocent. There is a fear that you won't be supported by management.

In addition to the two fears distinguished above workers also fear their own internal desire for retaliation which, as will be seen later, can assume the force of a murderous rage. On occasions the timely intervention of a colleague was necessary to remind a worker that they had momentarily lost control and needed to regain this before they acted in a way they would later regret:

I was in a tent lying with my back to a girl who kept kicking me in the kidneys for an hour. I kept telling her to stop it but she wouldn't and I went 'Bang!' I picked her up by the neck and I was lifting her…a colleague whispered, 'Just stop it!' and that was enough.

A young person chucked a phone at me and it hit my head. Then it was like a light being switched on, 'He's abusing you.' I pushed him against a wall and a member of staff kept saying, 'Let go of him' and I said, 'I can't, I can't…'

Once again a process of dissociation (Sinason 2002) can be seen at work. The worker's normally appropriate 'professional self' is lost or abandoned and a heedless, raging self takes over. This self has no regard for consequences. It is as if workers are literally blinded by their rage as they cannot comprehend why someone would want to harm them when they are there to help that young person. A feeling of 'How *dare* you do this to me!' sweeps over them, leaving no room for reflection or recognition of the course they are embarking upon. In the first of the two examples above a cautionary word from a colleague was sufficient to show the worker what he was doing and assist him in stopping this. In the second example it seems as if the worker recognizes the good advice she is being given but feels too much in the thrall of the raging self to free herself from it: 'I can't, I can't…'

Sometimes workers are unable to restrain themselves from acting on their desire for retaliation and there are no helpful colleagues nearby to stop them either:

> I was a residential social worker in a community home with education and was working with my wife. I came on to an afternoon shift just as my wife was finishing a morning shift. Just as I arrived on duty I saw someone pick up a shoe and hit my wife in the face. I merely saw red, grabbed hold of this person, dragged them down three flights of stairs and opened the headmaster's door with his head. I was approached later by the deputy who said that this was a serious assault and that there would be a formal inquiry.

The 'red mist' of anger descends and the worker is unable to see beyond the desire for retaliation which demands satisfaction. Van Heeswyk (1998) argues that young people can, perhaps unknowingly, encourage residential staff to act out violent relationships with them. Consequently workers are disturbed to discover aspects of themselves they might previously have been unaware of, let alone admitted:

> A child…may understand her removal to a residential setting as a punishment for having been bad. She may then see the workers as some sort of prison guards or as stern and frightening figures who are charged with exacting retribution. The workers may represent in the child's mind the abusing or neglectful parents of her early years… The workers may be shocked to find themselves ignored, retreated from or attacked and, worse still, may be horrified to find themselves experiencing hostile and violent feelings and thoughts towards the children. Workers may worry that they are, in fact, no better than the children's parents, of whom they were, hitherto, so critical. It is alarming and disturbing of one's composure and self-esteem to be put in touch with a violent and uncaring part of oneself and this significant concomitant of work with rejected, abused and deprived young people is a major source of stress for residential staff. (Van Heeswyk 1998, pp.76–77)

Mattingly (1981) points out the discrepancy between the acknowledged importance of the child care worker's role and the relatively low pay and status that the work commands. She claims that disillusionment seeps into the heart and soul of a worker's motivation, leaving him questioning his identity and purpose:

> ...while being told of his importance, and encouraged toward professional associations and training, [the residential child care worker] is deprived of the economic and psychological circumstances necessary to engage in an exciting and productive career...there is an inescapable stress producing conflict between the worker's commitment to give and the reality that frequently he cannot give enough...workers are confronted by assaultive youth, messy and aggressive children and ungrateful families. The nobility of caring work turns out to be a myth...the worker often comes to the conclusion that he is unfit for the work he has chosen. A severe fracture of professional identity is a common result. (Mattingly 1981, pp.154–157)

People are not attracted to residential work in health and social care because of the financial rewards or high status such work attracts. Their motivation is often rooted in personal experiences which they are frequently attempting to address vicariously through the work (Van Heeswyk 1998). To find oneself fundamentally unsuited to or unable to continue in a role which entails such a high level of personal investment can be a devastating blow with profound repercussions for identity and self-esteem. For some the fracturing of professional identity is so profound they are unable to continue working in residential care (Smith 1999). Sometimes a worker's indignation is such that harming a young person who threatens him is not sufficient. He wants to kill him. One residential worker said:

> You are dealing with very powerful emotions when you have been assaulted...you feel so angry that someone has hit you when you are trying to help them and it is this real anger that you cannot deal with. Yes, you can understand it, yes, you know why, yes, you know it's transference – but it's the feelings of real rage...you cannot bring that to supervision. I have wanted to kill – I have felt so angry – that if they were here now I would really want to do them damage...that is the bit that is not addressed...there is no reason good enough in my mind for hitting somebody. I do not care whether you look like their mother or whether you have said something that slightly upsets them.

This worker articulates the extreme rage ('fight' response) that can be experienced in response to someone seen as posing an unacceptable threat.

She shows how one can be equipped with the tools of understanding yet still feel that there is a justification of a kind for retaliation nonetheless.

A head of home with many years' experience of dealing with and responding to the type of fears illustrated in this chapter described how quickly fears of death could come to the fore of her mind:

> I fear that a member of staff will kill a young person. We've all flipped and it's to do with stress. I once had a fraught call saying, 'Come into the unit' and I saw a police car. It was a nice evening, really quiet. My fear was of what had happened. It was eerily quiet and I thought, 'Oh my God! They're all dead on the floor!' When I got there the incident was finished, they were all having a cup of tea and laughing and I didn't need to come in after all. But I do have a fear of coming into work and finding that someone has died, staff or resident. I don't think that I'll finish my career without someone dying.

Recommendations for practice and training

- The influence of 'the gothic' on the way that workers encapsulate and recall fear-provoking experiences should be acknowledged.

- The likelihood for even highly trained, skilled and experienced workers to forget what they know when frightened should be anticipated.

- The tendency for the care-taking self to temporarily take charge and look after the traumatized self when traumas are at their height should be recognized. Time and provision for de-briefing after the event should be made available.

- The fact that behaviours of service users can change suddenly, leaving workers to face threatening possibilities cut off from the assistance of colleagues, should be remembered.

- Policies should be in place for the reporting of dangerous incidents for Health and Safety monitoring purposes and for making contact with the police both during and after incidents.

- Workers' experiences of a desire to retaliate and hurt and even kill service users as a consequence of being traumatized should be acknowledged and addressed.

- Some workers will experience a 'fracture of professional identity' and the potentially profound consequences of this in terms of their mental health and self-image should be appreciated.

Chapter 6

Complaints, Bureaucracies and Workplace Bullying

Introduction

This chapter begins with examples of ways in which complaints can fundamentally undermine a worker's faith in themselves by re-awakening child-like feelings of guilt, shame and incompetence. Workers might have little faith in their seniors' ability to investigate complaints appropriately or fairly to the extent that some would prefer to be faced with threats of violence to being complained about, given the choice. The importance of managers acting as strong containers for anxiety in the workplace is then considered along with examples of when this has and has not been provided. The case of *Walker* v. *Northumberland County Council* (see Davies 1998) and the Climbié inquiry are discussed in the context of stress and fear in organizations. Examples of buildings and entire organizational systems being under fear-provoking threat are given. Finally, workplace bullying and different assessments of fear and risk by workers and managers are considered in the light of the Health and Safety at Work Act 1974.

Fears of complaints

Over recent years users of health and social care services have been increasingly encouraged to complain if they are not satisfied with the nature or level of service they receive. While this trend has welcome aspects as abuses have previously been perpetrated in secret and service users silenced too easily (Hunt 1995, 1998) the pendulum now seems to have swung so far in the other direction that complaints are sometimes used as a 'vindictive and/or mischievous' device to attack innocent staff (Webb and McCaffrey 1998, p.167). Townsend (1998, p.129) refers to service users who 'make a hobby of complaining' and suggests that some public inquiries can be seen as socially sanctioned, protracted and expensive complaints into social work, promoting a 'blame culture' which undermines professional competence and esteem.

A social worker recalled her experience of being complained about:

> I came back to dictate my notes from a difficult visit to a client's mother who shrieked at me down the telephone saying that I had broken confidentiality and that she was going to lodge a complaint against me which she subsequently did. I hadn't been complained about previously and did experience a real sense of fear which was about being confronted by my manager with something that impinged on my practice. A real, somehow genuine, fear, going over in my mind's eye, what did I say? What did I do? It was quite a primitive fear about being accused, at some very simple level of having done something bad. You've been bad, somebody is saying bad things about you. It's as primitive as that...it's child-like, you've done something bad and will have to face the consequences. In rational terms I didn't think that anything dreadful was going to happen to me but I was afraid.

Unfounded accusations of health and social care workers can cause profound damage to careers. People are frequently suspended and forbidden contact with colleagues while an accusation is investigated, leaving them cut off from the group to which they previously belonged and thus evoking heightened separation anxiety (see Chapter One). While suspensions are necessary in order for inquiries to be conducted there is an implicit suspicion that those accused are guilty until proved innocent, otherwise why can they not remain at work? This has a profound impact on those suspended. Grant (2003, p. 6) writes:

> More than one in four suspended hospital doctors has seen a psychiatrist because of their plight and more than one in ten has contemplated suicide... Of 105 suspended doctors surveyed, 27 per cent said that suspension had caused them to see a psychiatrist, 32 per cent to take medication and 13 per cent had felt suicidal.

Even when people are investigated and found not guilty they nonetheless emerge from investigation somehow tainted and damaged. 'Mud sticks' and there is said to be 'no smoke without fire'. In Shakespeare's *Othello* [1603] (1987, p.71) Cassio protests, 'Reputation, reputation, reputation! I have lost the immortal part of myself, and what remains is bestial. My reputation, Iago, my reputation!' Once people have died or finished work at a certain place their reputation 'lives on'. Fears of one's reputation being compromised or tarnished by complaints are therefore very real.

The fear of accusation evokes child-like responses of guilt and shame (see Chapter Five). The social worker quoted above recognizes that she is not worried 'in *rational* [i.e. adult] terms' but feels afraid nonetheless (by implication in non-rational i.e. more child-like terms). She continues, recalling her feelings while the complaint against her is being investigated:

> There is a part of one that is lost out there – which is being examined. To some extent it feels like being burgled. Somebody is going through things that are yours, that is 'you'. It's out there for the general public to do with it what it will, like a novel or a piece of poetry…being spread out on a table in front of those people.

The child-like embarrassment and shame of being exposed in front of others and the accompanying vulnerability this prompts is apparent in this quotation. The worker experiences a sense of intrusion, even violation as she describes herself as being 'spread out' in front of others, 'lost' to herself. She moves from describing records of her actions as being something that is hers (a possession) to something that is her (identity). She feels like a work of art, looked at, examined, analysed, construed, constructed and discussed by others, embodying possibilities of various interpretations and different de-constructions. She is concerned that, in her absence, someone will construe a version of her that she does not recognize and cannot accept.

A similar fear of being misconstrued and misinterpreted was voiced by a community nurse, this time in response to a complaint from a colleague rather than a service user:

> I was rude to a colleague as he was being petty. He sent in a written report about the incident and I had to respond to that. All that happened because of some leave I wanted, not so much for me, but for my wife who worked with this guy. He put in a complaint against me and I had to write

a report in defence of myself and I was due to go away. It's the 'no control'. You have some control – you write your report, you seek advice and all that but despite that you still feel things can turn against you... Some people go to court, they are the victim, but the whole thing could turn against them.

Once again, the fear of being misrepresented in one's absence is apparent. The nurse regards himself as the victim of his colleague's pettiness but is concerned, while he is not there to defend himself, things will turn against him and he will be cast in the role of the persecutor.

Another community nurse told of how he feared that a complaint made in response to an uncharacteristic and momentary lapse could ruin his career:

I was dealing with this woman who is known to be a pain in the backside but you can't tell her that because of the relationship. I did put the phone down on that woman which I never do, or rarely do, and I probably said some unkind words as well. She said, 'I'm going to put in a complaint about you.' The fear is that the one moment you react, that's it, it will be used to say, 'That's you.'

Fears arising from being complained about can be so profound that, given a choice, workers might prefer the threat of a violent assault to being complained about:

A man was being verbally abusive, pointing his finger, f'ing and blinding. I wanted his child to be examined. I was afraid that he would make complaints about me and was afraid of the reaction of management if he did. I was also afraid that he was going to hit me; or something worse – kill me. It was intensely difficult for seven weeks. He was a violent man with a criminal record and I would dream of the family threatening me. I began to dream that the man was following me, that he held me prisoner, at knifepoint and stabbed me. The family made complaints about me that chipped away at my confidence. It wasn't the complaints they made as much as the way they were handled that made it difficult. I'm more frightened when I'm in my work office than I am when out visiting people. It's the criticisms of your practice internally that are the most difficult. You feel you can't do anything right. The people who deal with complaints haven't a clue about what we're doing. It's got worse recently. I'm happier when visiting clients, even that difficult one, compared to the fear that I feel in the office. I went off work for five weeks with stress and fear.

This worker presents a composite fear of being assaulted, being killed, and being complained about. Bearing in mind the lack of confidence she voices in her own management's ability to respond appropriately to complaints against her it is interesting that she dreams of the *family* making complaints about her that chipped away at her confidence. Her statement that she is more frightened when in her office than she is when out visiting clients, even those who might threaten her with violence and possibly death, is indicative of the level of fear which threats and complaints can inspire. Her faith in the understanding and ability of her managers to deal with the complaint against her is negligible. If threatened with violence rather than a complaint, at least her defence would be more 'in her own hands', under her control, rather than in the control of someone else she does not trust. Perhaps this is why she implies she would prefer to be threatened with violence than complained about.

Managers, however, might also fear being complained about. A male manager said:

> Because of my management style I fear getting set up. A colleague of mine lost his job in 1991 when political correctness was just starting to take control and there were no boundaries as to what sexual harassment was. Two women set him up and accused him of group and individual sexual harassment even though there was no physical contact or direct approach involved. It was based on perceived innuendo. There were no preliminary warnings. He was instantly dismissed. I recently read that one of the women had made an allegation of attempted rape against someone else. This was thrown out of court and she was strongly criticized. I could be placed in a setting where a complaint is made and managers need to sort it out. I don't trust their ability to distinguish between fantasy and fiction. They're more concerned with window dressing and image than justice in the department...

This manager echoes the concern voiced by the social worker quoted above, that he has no confidence in the ability of his seniors to respond to a complaint with appropriate understanding. Once again, there is the fear of accusation by way of malicious complaint and the recognition that complaints processes might be used by complainants pursuing additional agendas. Whatever the reasons for the complaint, being complained about evokes considerable vulnerability, and, with it, anxiety.

Managers' responses to complaints: the containment of anxiety

Whilst service users should be entitled to complain about poor, inappropriate or even abusive practice it is unrealistic to expect service providers to be perfect. Even the most motivated, highly trained, well-regarded and widely experienced workers will not get everything right all of the time. Little allowance is made for human frailty or imperfection within the health and social care workforce and workers are therefore in an impossible position: charged with getting it right all the time, while knowing simultaneously that this can never be achieved. The desire to retaliate is part of being human and sometimes workers might even feel hatred towards those they work with (Winnicott 1987). (The dilemma posed for residential workers who feel like hurting those in their care is discussed in Chapter Five.) Fears of justified complaints which might expose human weakness and unjustified complaints which might be used maliciously are therefore very potent. Managers can be regarded as a threat, rather than a support, in such instances.

In needing someone to blame and not being able to blame the service users workers might use managers as scapegoats, projecting into them their partly recognized discontent concerning being complained about:

> Since emotions in the staff group are likely to mirror those felt by the deprived and abused young people themselves, there is a further danger that a vicious circle will ensue in which the workers pass on to their managers their own version of the troubled complaints and states of mind that they have been experiencing from those in their care. Deprived people can put us in touch with our own feelings or phantasies of deprivation. In these circumstances it can be easy to hold supervisors and employers responsible for our discontent, those whose task, we feel, is to protect and provide for ourselves. (Van Heeswyk 1998, p.77)

Menzies-Lyth, in her famous study of nursing 'The functioning of social systems as a defence against anxiety' (in Menzies-Lyth 1992), claimed that seniors and managers were often aware of difficulties experienced by junior staff but were unable to communicate this awareness because of the repressive nature of the system in which they worked:

> ...students are wrong when they say that senior nurses do not understand or feel for their distress. In personal conversations with us, seniors showed considerable understanding and sympathy and often remembered surprisingly vividly some of the agonies of their own training. But they lacked confidence in their ability to handle emotional stress in any way other than by repressive techniques... Kindly, sympathetic handling of emotional stress between staff and student nurses is, in any case, inconsistent with traditional nursing roles and relationships, which require repression, discipline and reprimand from senior to junior. (Menzies-Lyth 1992, p.54)

Obholzer and Roberts (1994, p.174) suggest that focusing on budgets instead of patient/service-user pain is a classic example of managers protecting themselves from the emotional distress they know the work to entail yet do not want to experience. Alongside this distancing process Menzies-Lyth claimed that nurses would also split off aspects of themselves and project them into others, irresponsibility into juniors and severity into seniors:

> Each nurse tends to split off aspects of herself from her conscious personality and to project them into other nurses. Her irresponsible impulses, which she fears she cannot control, are attributed to her juniors. Her painfully severe attitude to these impulses and burdensome sense of responsibility are attributed to her seniors. Consequently, she identifies juniors with her irresponsible self and treats them with the severity that self is felt to deserve. Similarly, she identifies seniors with her own harsh disciplinary attitude to her irresponsible self and expects harsh discipline. (Menzies-Lyth 1992, p.57)

Nurses, and others in the caring professions, are at risk of being flooded by intense anxieties which threaten to overwhelm and therefore have to be managed. Minimizing their importance and projecting them into others are ways of responding to them by defending against them. Full confrontation is thought to be too risky, threatening personal disruption and social chaos (Menzies-Lyth 1992, pp.63,78). The difficulties for staff attempting to deal successfully with their individual anxieties are compounded by the fact that the large institutions in which they work (e.g. hospitals and social care departments) function as containers for fundamental human anxieties. As well as their own anxieties, therefore, workers are also contending with the confused and compounded anxieties of others, and attempting to separate out which anxieties belong to whom. The irrational, confusing and contagious aspects of fear make this task far from straightforward.

Managers can also be victims of extreme fear-provoking situations and, as a consequence, need sympathetic and appropriate help from their own managers. In the ground-breaking case of *Walker* v. *Northumberland County Council* in 1995 Walker's employers were found negligent of their duty of care to him. Walker was a child care manager who suffered a breakdown as the result of over-work. Returning to work he was promised a reduced workload and additional help. Neither was forthcoming and Walker suffered a second breakdown. His employers were found liable for his second breakdown. While it was recognized that they might not have foreseen his first breakdown, it was thought that they should have anticipated the second and taken reasonable steps to prevent this which they did not take. The employers were found liable on the grounds that the breakdown was both intrinsic to Walker's work and foreseeable. They ought to have anticipated the second breakdown in the context of the first.

The inquiry into the death of Victoria Climbié (Laming 2003) is unusual in its recognition of the part played (or not played) by management which contributed to Victoria's death. In previous child death inquiries front-line social workers have frequently been singled out for blame (see Chapter Two). Laming is unusual in emphasizing the need for managers to be seen to be accountable for the performance, and the accompanying stresses and fears, of their staff. His report shows that organizations as well as individuals can be infused with anxiety.

Organizations under threat

Sometimes threats will be made to organizations and buildings rather than individuals and siege situations develop as described in the following quotations:

> A client came in, demanding to see a social worker. The client wouldn't go away. It got near to closing time and the client still refused to leave. They went to their car to get something and a senior officer decided to

lock the door and then there was a siege situation. The client was outside, throwing bricks and stones at the building and the staff couldn't get out.

Some people had settled in an area and a social worker had to visit and remove a child from them. The people were angry and had threatened to come and get the child back. The police instructed the staff to lock themselves in for safety. We were all frightened and yet we found the incident exciting. The situation was quickly defused.

In the first example an attempt at firm containment and adhering to strict boundaries (i.e. the closing time of the office) seems to have resulted in escalating fears and their repercussions rather than subduing them. In the second example the excitement which is often a near neighbour to fear is apparent. Workers have also been fearful when they have unearthed what lies beneath an organizational veneer of respectability:

I was a team leader at a hospital and my hair stood on end about the social work practice within the team and the amount of conflict and strife which was unbelievable. The secretarial staff was hopeless beyond belief. I thought, 'What have I done?' I battled with it all and began to uncover what was going on in paediatrics, accident and emergency and child protection, or, more accurately, what wasn't going on. There were some very worrying situations not being addressed in any way whatsoever. I feared that the team dynamics would get out of control; they were already out of control. I feared their hostility to me. Child protection was an absolute fiasco. I thought, 'If I can see this, and it isn't my speciality, what the hell are they all doing?' I kept waking with terrible premonitions of doom and couldn't get back to sleep. I went to my GP who wanted to give me anti-depressants. I said, 'I'm not depressed, I'm frightened' – it was horrible.

This worker's description combines a sense of impossible unreality with inescapable truth in a surreal cocktail. She literally cannot believe how bad things are and yet knows it to be true. Her comments reveal an organizational malaise, a system permeated with anxiety, riddled to the core. She fears something terrible will happen and that she will be found at least partly responsible. She knows she has the option of whistle blowing but there are considerable inhibitors to this (Hunt 1995, 1998). She internalizes the organization's anxiety and, like the worker quoted above, finds her fears in her dreams as her unconscious, as well as her conscious, mind struggles to cope. Like scapegoats in families individual workers will often carry and manifest an organization's problems. The GP's offer of anti-depressants to some extent focuses upon the worker as being or having the problem, rather than the organization, and is therefore not felt to be appropriate or experienced as helpful.

Workers might look to managers to contain anxiety but find those managers to be only too human, with fears and anxieties of their own. Managers' fears can feed contagious aspects of the anxiety so that fears grow larger rather than diminish:

> A client was in a street agency, a methadone clinic. He couldn't have looked meaner – a skinhead with a big Alsatian dog on a chain; the epitome of nastiness really. He couldn't see the doctor, was not happy about this, and let us know it. He had to wait. He calmed down but the manager over-reacted. She ran off and hid. She asked, 'Should we call the police?' It took as much to calm her down as the client, if not more. She could easily have set him off again. She said later, 'We've got to review safety policies; we've all got to have mobile phones'… It wasn't necessary. It was an over-reaction and really unhelpful.

This quotation illustrates one of the difficulties in finding an appropriate level of response to fear. One needs to be sufficiently afraid to take notice and act appropriately, but not so fearful that one becomes paralysed and overwhelmed by the fear. To some extent, managers are like their social workers, damned if they do, and damned if they don't. If they do not take action they could be accused of being too casual and insufficiently concerned about the level of danger their workers face. If they do take action, this could be objected to on the grounds that it was not needed and has unnecessarily complicated, or even exacerbated, an already difficult situation. Any person's fear about any particular situation relates as much to re-awakened fears from past experiences as to the current threat faced. This particular manager might have experienced a previous trauma involving a dog, for example, so that no matter how proficient she was in her role, she would have been disabled by the memory of the previous trauma. Most workers are unlikely to know their colleagues' 'trauma histories' in detail and so cannot be aware of the full repercussions of subjective memories and their associated effects.

An example of a manager providing a welcome containing of anxiety was provided by a receptionist who had experienced a violent service user smashing his way through a reception area in search of a social worker he wanted to attack. The receptionist is describing a 'de-briefing' meeting held after the event to consider what lessons could be learned for the future:

> I did voice my feelings to a manager in charge. She was good and listened. I was afraid that I would go to work and never come back as there was a threat that this guy would go to court and be released and that next time he would come back and finish us all off. We had a meeting in the building with all departments. It was well attended and I spoke up. By going to the meeting and speaking I felt I was doing something positive. I said I thought the reception area should be reinforced. We live in violent times and we get all sorts of people in. It has been made better now. There's an intercom so that reception can sift through callers.

In contrast to the previous example this worker feels securely 'held' and appropriately contained by her manager following a serious threat at her place of work. Following a disconcerting experience the worker's imagination feeds her fears to the extent that she envisages being killed at work along with all of her colleagues ('the next time he would…finish us all off'). Although this is unlikely it is indicative of the extent to which fears grow in the mind once fuelled by the imagination. Being listened to initially, and seeing action taken as a result of her expressed concern, gives the receptionist confidence in her manager. The response of the manager and organization is such that the fear is allayed. While unconditional and guaranteed re-assurance can never be genuinely given in such instances the worker feels satisfied that her concerns have been heard, noted and acted upon. She recognizes that there is not much more that a manager can do in such circumstances and begins to feel a sense of control re-established. She felt she was doing something positive in being part of the solution rather than part of the problem. A regained sense of control is of great importance following fear-provoking experiences as it is often the loss of control that is experienced as particularly fearful.

Sometimes a worker's loss of control is experienced as a result of being bullied in the workplace. This topic is now considered.

Workplace bullying

A residential worker recalled:

> I feared my boss. What she could do. I could lose my job if I didn't conform. She would make my life hell if I didn't do what she asked. She ruled by fear; the power of the pen. She would put 'Staff please note' in red ink in the log book. I was a threat to her as I progressed. She phoned the college threatening my placement when I was qualifying. She had to be in control. I was young and up-and-coming. I asked too many questions, tried to introduce new methods. She would say, 'I'm in charge. Don't question things or upset the apple cart because I know people in high places.' It was worse because we were 'residential' workers – we lived in. I felt sick in the pit of my stomach, waiting on Sunday nights, shaking from head to foot, knowing that the next few seconds would determine what kind of a shift I was going to have. If I was greeted with, 'Hello love, I'm in the kitchen' I knew it would be all right. If there was a deathly silence I knew it wouldn't be.

This worker's fear is all the more potent because she depended on her job for her accommodation. Were she to lose her job she would be homeless. She conveys her fear concerning the power that bosses such as hers used to have and how this power could be used against those regarded as a threat or if the manager was in a bad mood. Workplace bullying remains a matter of concern for workers today (Clifton and Serdar 2003) and might take a more subtle form than in the example above as illustrated in the following quotation when a worker reported that she did not like:

> ...being told that I am worried for no reason – my manager saying, 'That would have been perfectly OK. What do you mean, you don't want to visit them at home?' Invalidating the way that I feel. I'm not 21 and impressionable. If I say I'm scared, I'm scared and I don't scare easy.

Under the Health and Safety at Work Act 1974 employers have a responsibility to take all reasonable steps to promote the health, safety and wellbeing of their employees. Employees have a responsibility to co-operate with their employers in this duty and not to expose themselves to unnecessary risks. There might, therefore, be differences of opinion about what is sufficiently safe. A manager, removed from the recent realities of practice, might instruct a worker to carry out a home visit alone whereas the worker might regard the visit as too risky. Subtle, or not so subtle, pressure could be brought to bear on the worker resulting in her feeling bullied into doing something against her better judgement, rather than consulted as a co-construer of risk as required by the Health and Safety at Work Act. The influence of different individuals' prior exposure to or denial of similar fear-provoking experiences on decision making, as mentioned previously in this chapter, also needs to be acknowledged. Different weights are commonly given to differently expressed differences of opinion. In the example just quoted a manager might claim that they were merely suggesting an alternative way of assessing a risk but for the worker concerned it felt more than this and communicated an invalidation of the way she felt.

Recommendations for practice and training

- The profound, disabling and child-like feelings of guilt, shame and incompetence that might be experienced by workers as a consequence of being accused by means of complaints procedures should be recognized.

- Managers need to tread a fine line between under and over-reaction when their workers feel threatened. They will be seen ideally as 'strong containers' of anxiety yet able to act appropriately when need be.

- The possible tendency for workers to project feelings of irresponsibility into those 'beneath' them in the bureaucracy and harshness into those 'above' should be acknowledged.

- The dangers of avoiding emotional pain and focusing instead on budgets and performance indicators should be guarded against.

- Managers too should be protected from bureaucratic processes that take insufficient account of the intrinsic and foreseeable nature of stress arising from over-demanding workloads (as in the Walker case).

- The importance of managers being meaningfully accountable for their front-line staff as highlighted by the Climbié Inquiry should be recognized.

- The possibility of bureaucracies becoming dangerously out of control should be acknowledged and addressed.

- Policies should be in place to alert managers to workplace bullying and prevent this from happening or continuing.

Chapter 7

What Helps? (1)

Colleagues, Supervision, Family

Introduction

This is the first of two chapters which consider what workers who have encountered fear-provoking experiences have found helpful when attempting to deal with these experiences. In particular, help given by colleagues, supervision and family members are considered in this chapter. Because these sources of support were of potential help to workers they were also, therefore, experienced as unhelpful at times and both helpful and unhelpful responses from colleagues, supervision and family members are illustrated. Colleagues working 'on the same level' as workers are shown as being particularly helpful in the aftermath of fear-provoking experiences primarily because they were available when wanted, did not pose the perceived threat of evaluation that a supervisor might, and are credited with understanding events. The qualities of a hypothetical 'ideal supervisor' with whom a worker might share a fear-provoking experience are itemized and illustrated. Internal and group supervision are considered in addition to 'one to one' sessions. A consideration of responses from family members concludes the chapter.

Sharing experiences with colleagues 'on the same level'

The item rated as most helpful by participants interviewed for research studies into both fear and stress was to be able to share what they had experienced with their peers – colleagues 'on the same level' as them. A residential worker suggests why this should be the case:

The staff become a community. It's about looking after each other. You want a staff team that's ideally open, as open as you can be; not 'counselling type' open but you can discuss issues you don't agree on if there's a feeling of an open agenda in a staff team. Of most help is the back-up of the staff – not particularly there and then. If you know you'll be supported in the morning, someone saying, 'Sit down, let me get you a cup of tea and I'll do the handover.' This is a really helpful thing.

It is apparent from previous chapters how people contend with the pain of being separated from the social group that they want to belong to and the subsequent fears of annihilation that these fears can give rise to. To feel that a sense of community has been re-established and that one's place within that community is affirmed and welcomed by others is powerful in its healing. Another worker also makes this point, highlighting the welcome relief of feeling 'de-isolated':

I'm helped by honest feelings and feedback from members of the team. It de-isolates you someone saying, 'I would have felt the same' or, 'There was no need for you to have been frightened, I wouldn't have been.' It's not the agreement or disagreement that is helpful but the honesty that helps. Colleagues can help me not to be afraid.

The participant is saying here that they are really seeking *connection* rather than agreement. Again, the sense of being returned to the fold is apparent. Another worker saw the support from peers as forming a kind of cumulative pool over the years which could be drawn from at times of need:

You're helped by discussion, history, information and advice. All the support you've had over the years from different people. Things they've shared with you, how they've supported you and given advice; you can pool that – it's like a history of all that you've retained which you can remember at times like that.

Sometimes colleagues were experienced as helpful because they made it possible for participants to go on from talking to them to then being able to talk with their senior:

The nice thing is that you've got colleagues and people you can turn to. You know the support's there. You've been told that it's there, and it is. After a difficult time my colleague came up and gave me a hug and made me a cup of tea. I could then talk to my senior. This is the beauty of the support available.

Although English people are sometimes ridiculed for making cups of tea at times of crisis it is interesting how these have featured in some participants' recollections of particularly supportive responses from colleagues! One of the reasons why colleagues were so often favoured over managers as an initial source of support following traumatic experiences was that they were frequently perceived as being less likely to judge:

> Talking to colleagues and peer support is the most helpful. This is better than talking with line management as you can explore your practice without judgement. Managers look at things from an accountability/complaints point of view, 'Have you done everything right?' Peers can explore without judgement.

Workers might be particularly reluctant to expose their deepest fears, weaknesses and vulnerabilities to seniors who are responsible for writing appraisals, evaluations and references. While people are liable to regret having shared a confidence with anyone who can later carry or represent that memory for them this was a particular concern in relation to managers. One worker who respected her supervisor and enjoyed a good relationship with her said, 'However well you think you get on with your supervisor, once you tell them something, it's there to return.' As well as being less likely to judge a worker (at least in a professional development or complaints procedure sense) colleagues were more likely than supervisors to be immediately available to share distressing experiences. For workers whose supervisors were not based in the same office as they were and/or were committed to meetings much in advance, to make an appointment to talk would introduce elements of formality and delay which were often not wanted. In addition, colleagues were often seen as having credibility necessary for understanding and as knowing the current reality of the work being engaged in it themselves. Even so, colleagues were not perceived as always helpful.

Unhelpful responses from colleagues

Just as colleagues were experienced as potentially extremely helpful they could also compound feelings of fear, isolation and inadequacy at times.

One worker had just completed a telephone call with a service user who was threatening suicide. The worker was alarmed by this and felt concern and a sense of responsibility. She shared this concern with a colleague who said, dismissively, 'Oh her – she's always saying that.' This was not helpful to the worker who felt that her concerns had been tactlessly under-estimated by her colleague's response.

Another female participant had been surprised by a man grabbing her arm in a dark and remote location. She feared she might be assaulted or worse. The impact of this incident was such that it resulted in her giving up work at nights. When the incident was discussed at a meeting however, she recalls a colleague reporting it as, 'A gentleman asked if he could have a lift – make sure you all carry torches.' This completely under-estimated and misrepresented the nature and extent of fear she had felt.

Sometimes workers experienced themselves as being in competition with one another and fear-provoking experiences could be used as a means of pushing others down the hierarchy:

> It's unhelpful when another worker says that they've never been assaulted, you've obviously done something wrong. They create a feeling that you're to blame, not experienced, there's something in you lacking that made you the victim. It wouldn't have happened to them. They're trying to build themselves up at your expense, as if they're better than you. What this worker has said has stuck with me. I lacked support from this worker when I needed support. I used to respect them and I don't any more.

Clearly, a response such as this is unhelpful. The feeling of being seen in the victim role as a consequence of one's shortcomings and inadequacies contrasts with the liberating and helpful aspects of recognizing that one has been victim-ized which has been discussed earlier in this chapter.

Supervisors, particularly if they had not practised in the same work area as participants (recently or at all), were sometimes not credited with being able to understand what it is *really* like. Despite these (often inevitable) limitations of the supervisory role several participants had found it helpful to share their experiences with their supervisor.

Supervision

Supervision has been an established feature of social work and counselling practice since their earliest days (Hawkins and Shohet 1990; Hughes and Pengelly 1998; Mattinson 1975; Shipton 1997; Westheimer 1977). The practice of supervision has its roots in the psychoanalytic tradition and the belief that those attempting to understand and help others should themselves be understood and helped. Supervision should aid self-awareness and enable practitioners to become more able to identify their own limitations and incompletely worked-through experiences so that these do not hinder or frustrate their attempts to help others. It should also play a part in teaching skills and improving technique. In addition, it is a mechanism by which agencies can maintain some quality control with regard to the work that goes on in their name and ensure that they can be appropriately accountable for such work.

Supervision is of such importance to health and social care work that a separate question was asked specifically about it in the research study inquiring into experiences of fear (see Introduction), when participants were asked what responses they would like from an 'ideal supervisor' with whom they shared a fear-provoking experience. Most desired was that supervisors would *'be there' for them and have time to listen to them without judgement or criticism.* One participant said they wanted a supervisor:

> …to listen and let you get it off your chest. You don't want to tell every-body, just one person. You just want to unload without feeling uncom-fortable, knowing that it's not going any further unless it's something that needs action.

This participant speaks of a need to get rid of something ('unload', 'get it off your chest') and have it safely held and contained. Particularly in the immediate aftermath of trauma people are not able to analyse or discuss what they can learn from experiences, they just want to be rid of them, distance/separate themselves from them and 'get back' to their pre-traumatized selves. The value of sharing what has happened with just one person rather than diluting the effectiveness of response by talking with several people is highlighted here. This contrasts with the potential value of a range of perspectives that is made possible by group rather than individual supervision and which is discussed below. Reviewing research conducted into a supervision policy in a social services department

Froggett (2000) comments that the most significant factor for supervisees influencing the outcome of supervision was the quality of their relationship with their supervisor. While those who enjoyed a mutually satisfactory relationship with their supervisor might be pleased to share fear-provoking experiences with that one person, those who did not would experience this as unhelpful, even counter-productive, rather than helpful.

An experienced worker did not want her several years of experience to prevent her supervisor from realizing that she needed understanding and support despite her expertise:

> Perhaps supervisors are guilty of thinking that qualified workers have got their act together. A supervisor needs to listen out for what they're not being told as well as what they are told. They could ask, 'How are you dealing with the work? How is the work impinging on you?' and not just, 'Has she paid her electricity bill?'... The person needs to be heard before the social worker.

It seems easier, less painful, and therefore arguably preferable to concentrate on measurable practicalities rather than disturbing, threatening and ultimately unquantifiable feelings in the aftermath of fear-provoking experiences. The current emphasis on performance measurement and 'star ratings' that are affecting health and social care departments entails the danger of minimizing or missing altogether the crucial human aspects of the work. Cooper (2000) argues that a logic of control and inspection are forcing out a logic of compassion and development from the provision of welfare, and with regard to supervision in particular Frogget (2000, pp.27–32) writes of:

> ...a national trend towards a managerialist preoccupation with systems of information, monitoring and control... Fear of error seemed to grip whole teams for a while, hindering their ability to see supervision as anything other than an exhausting addition to procedural hurdles.

The checking and monitoring aspects of supervision seem to be threatening to choke the life out of the supportive, nurturing and enhancing aspects and this is precisely what workers who have experienced fear do not want. The fear of error mentioned by Froggett was illustrated by an officer in charge of a residential unit who said, 'Some of the staff are a bit funny about supervision – they look on it as something that happens when they've done something wrong.'

Another experienced social worker wanted:

> To be properly listened to in an unbiased way by somebody even if they don't agree with you. You can feel instinctively that there are some who will warp your story and not listen.

This quotation illustrates what Mattinson (1975) called the 'mirroring' effect whereby the difficulties, dynamics and dilemmas (sometimes represented by the same words and phrases) in the casework relationship between practitioner and service user also surface in the relationship between supervisor and supervisee. The worker had previously referred to the experience of fear as something that 'warped' her sense of self. Her concern here is that just as she feared her sense of self could be warped by the service user, her story could also be warped by a supervisor. Supervisors who were 'there' (present) for their supervisees and made time to listen to them without judgement were less likely to mirror unhelpful aspects of the casework relationship within the supervisory relationship.

Closely following qualities of 'being there' for supervisees, having time for them and listening to them without judgement, the 'ideal supervisor' would *understand, acknowledge, recognize and reflect.* One participant wanted her supervisor to:

> Really listen, to things not said as well as to what is said. I would like them to have some knowledge of my client's past and to have been there herself. I want her to accept my professional opinion, sympathize on a human level, and maybe let me go home an hour early.

Another:

> I feel supported if my supervisor has had some experience of social work. If she doesn't expect me to do things that she wasn't prepared to do herself and gave me a great deal of licence to involve her if I needed to. I want someone who is in touch with what I'm doing from day to day, someone who had a common understanding of what I was doing... As a social worker I feel too detached from my managers. It might be too strong to say that I have a fear that they wouldn't understand too easily. You want somebody who can understand fairly quickly.

Again, the importance in the supervisee's eyes of the supervisor having 'been there' himself as a route to *really* understanding is apparent. While some participants talked of a value in sharing experiences with supportive partners, family and friends (see below) for others these people were unlikely to be able to really understand the full impact of an experience as they inevitably lacked knowledge of the working environment, unlike the ideal supervisor:

> Supervision helps because you can go home and talk about an incident but the other person never 'really' knows. They can have an idea but they're not dealing with the same people in the same environment as the supervisor is.

Validation, affirmation, confirmation and support were the qualities next wanted from the ideal supervisor. Sometimes a brief acknowledgement from a supervisor was perceived to be powerful, even liberating, because it was so affirming and supportive. Examples include, 'My supervisor said afterwards that the client was psychotic and this was a great relief because I had felt trapped' and, 'I told my supervisor and she was outraged. She said, "You shouldn't have stayed there five minutes!"' Confirmation that the supervisee did all they reasonably could and making this known to others was appreciated by the next two participants:

> I want someone who will listen while you sound off, who will be supportive; someone who discusses what went on and helps you to realize that there's nothing else you could have done.

> A good supervisor is someone who takes a strong line in defence of their staff. It's great if someone is understanding and if they listen and don't think you're a wimp. But they need to take a strong line and stand up to the next person and say, 'And there's this, and this, and this...'

The fear of being perceived as inadequate as a consequence of a fear-provoking experience is notable in these accounts as is the desire for a 'strong protector' who acts like a supportive parent-figure and fights the supervisee's cause on the necessary fronts.

For one participant the affirmation of herself she wanted entailed willingness on the part of the supervisor to look at and think about the primitive and disturbing aspects of fear and not retreat into offering superficial reassurance:

> I would like someone who is not afraid to address the very primitive feelings that fear arouses. They may be afraid of fear for themselves but they're not afraid of examining it in somebody else. Someone who is able

to address the very painful and worrying feelings is the best. Those who are not so good use the more kind of reassuring techniques which help less.

Supervision was seen to be of crucial importance and potential help both as preparation for and in the aftermath of fear-provoking experiences. One social worker participant in the research into fear commented:

> I agreed to talk to you as I think supervision is fundamental to what we do. Good supervision isn't just about seeing that the files are up to date or making sure that the social worker hasn't dropped a clanger... We involve ourselves in dangerous situations and we're such a despised profession. My interest is more in the 'supervision' aspects of your research than the 'fear' aspects.

Thus far this discussion has focused mainly on the traditional method of casework supervision of social workers which is typically carried out by way of a one-to-one meeting between supervisor and supervisee. Before leaving the helpful aspects of supervision internal and group supervision are now briefly considered.

Internal supervision and group supervision

The term 'internal supervision' has been coined by Casement (1985) to describe a process by which workers supervised themselves internally while actually engaged in interactions with others. Apart from rare instances when practitioners will be observed and heard working with service users by way of one-way mirrors and audio equipment (live supervision) most supervision of work takes place after the event and consists of the supervisee presenting the supervisor with edited highlights of exchanges that they have noticed, remembered and chosen to relate. Therefore, no matter how much the supervisee strives for an honest and fair representation of events in a supervision session even the most diligent and conscientious of workers is prey to the selectivity and inaccuracy of memory (see Ofshe and Watters 1995). Also, while supervision offers an opportunity to learn from experience and, to some extent, to plan ahead for future meetings, the supervisee is not usually able to consult with their supervisor while actually undertaking work with service users.

Casement's (1985) model of 'internal supervision' attempts to encapsulate the benefits of 'after-the-event' supervision and bring them forward so that they can be accessed at, and in, the time when worker and service user are together. The supervisor is therefore internalized and becomes a part of the supervisee's thinking. For example, a supervisor and supervisee might be reflecting on an occasion when the supervisee was taken hostage by a service user and reviewing what led up to this. He may consider, in retrospect, whether, or not, the supervisee could have detected early warning signs indicating what was to happen from the service user's behaviour. The supervisee says, 'Come to think of it, just before he locked me in, I thought he had a strange, far-away look in his eye, and this made me feel uneasy. However, I quickly dismissed this, thinking, "It's probably nothing..." Looking back I think I should have paid more attention to my intuition which was trying to protect me by alerting me to something unusual about his non-verbal communication'. The supervisor acknowledges this possibility.

The limitation of such an exchange is that the supervisee is inevitably wise after the event rather than before it or during it. If the supervisor is internalized the supervisee can have this inner dialogue as the event is unfolding and thus be better placed to influence its possible cause. A silent consultation with the internal supervisor might proceed along the following lines:

Service user: Why don't you sit down in that chair over there?

Worker: (thinks – he has a strange look in his eye which makes me feel uncomfortable – consults with internal supervisor) Why should that be?

Internal supervisor: What do you think? Could he be under the influence of substances or experiencing hallucinations or extremely preoccupied with something else? Either way I think you should be careful.

Worker: (replying to internal supervisor) Yes, come to think of it, I now recall that he took someone hostage a few years back. I'll make an excuse and leave. (Aloud to service user) I'm so sorry, I've just remembered something vital I need to attend to, will you excuse me today and I'll come back and see you another time?

The advantage of internal supervision is that it creates a thinking space at a time when carefully considering options could make a difference between being attacked and leaving safely. It offers a means by which the care-taking self can be accessed and employed to look after the traumatized self (see Chapters Two and Three), for an observing ego to offer helpful comments from its more distanced perspective to the functioning ego.

Sometimes social workers and counsellors, in particular, will be supervised in a group instead of individually. While groups inevitably lack the confidentiality and exclusive attention which one-to-one supervision meetings confer they can provide powerful and helpful reassurance for workers who feel validated by several peers who know them and their work:

> The supervision group was helpful and supportive. They believed me, they took on my feelings and said, 'There's no way you should carry on with this' and they supported me. They knew my strengths and that I could usually cope with difficult clients.

A counsellor reported:

> After explaining things to my group of colleagues they said that the client's behaviour was totally out of order. They affirmed me and gave me reassurance. It wasn't how 'I' had handled this man. The main part that was helpful was discussing it with colleagues. Re-affirming that I'd done the best that I could in that situation.

Perceived inappropriate responses from supervisors

Whereas supervisors were positively regarded when they acted as sympathetic containers of anxiety and strong protectors who helped mobilize the strength of the peer group, at times they seemed to do the opposite as this counsellor recalls:

> I had answered a client's question. My supervisor had written a book and thought that you should never answer questions. She didn't think that I should be working in a prison setting where I was frightened. The supervision group tried to perpetuate fear in me and make me experience more fear than I had. The supervisor reminded me of a disapproving mother, telling me that I shouldn't have these feelings.

Again, the supervisor is seen as a parent-figure but this time as critical, rather than nurturing/supportive. The peer group, so frequently described as being helpful to participants, is remembered here as reinforcing the supervisor's criticism and engendering fear rather than allaying it. Supervision has the potential for seeming fault-finding and undermining as well as being affirming and reassuring.

Another participant expressed frustration that she was not being heard at the level of her concern:

> Very often in supervision you talk about a concern and the response you get is, 'We'll look into that' but it doesn't happen. I don't think team managers are aware of this. Co-ordinators are not on the ball. They don't realize or they don't take what you're saying on board. 'How awful!' is the standard phrase. What would be helpful is being assured that co-ordinators would do something and would ensure that team managers get to know… I think it would be helpful to have a padded room where you can scream your head off. Co-ordinators are sympathetic but that doesn't help. Saying, 'Don't worry about it' is unhelpful. To me supervision is only for the purpose of discussing clients, not for discussing how I feel.

This quotation conveys the concern that those in positions of authority cannot be trusted to understand or act appropriately. Undertakings are given but not fulfilled; managers lack awareness; co-ordinators are not 'on the ball'. Neither fully realize what is happening and they do not take what is said 'on board' as they ought. Such is the lack of confidence in being appropriately understood that the participant prefers the idea of 'screaming her head off' (i.e. being cut off from thinking altogether) in a padded room to sharing an experience with her seniors. Attempts to reassure are seen as being trite, superficial and worthless.

It is understandable that workers should feel unacknowledged and inadequately appreciated when their seniors do not convey appropriate understanding. In some cases, however, seniors might make time for their workers and show concern yet be perceived as intrusive rather than helpful:

> I had a female senior who was young and into being very caring, very open. I found it difficult to be so exposed and open. She would say, 'And how are you? How are you *really*?' I dreaded it. You don't want to cry, especially as a fella with a female supervisor but when she said, '…and how's your mother?' (who was unwell at the time), I couldn't stop from crying. This was touching an emotional well that I didn't want touched. The supervisory work relationship is one too close to talk about these things. It wouldn't have been healthy – more disabling – to enter into it. I

didn't want to get that close with my line manager, I would feel too exposed. It's physically draining. You don't want to go into your place of work and find yourself on the floor.

In this quotation the participant describes behaviours from his supervisor that seem indicative of genuine interest and concern; she made time for him, showed interest in him, was open to what might lie beneath the surface, and made connections with his out-of-work life. In some ways these responses might seem to characterize the type of responses desired from an ideal supervisor rather than unhelpful responses. Yet, the participant 'dreaded it' and felt himself touched emotionally where he did not want to be touched. He felt disabled, rather than empowered, exposed rather than understood, physically drained, rather than lighter and stronger. The cumulative effect was that he feared being rendered incapable (on the floor) rather than assisted to carry on with his work.

One possible reason as to why this participant should be so adversely affected by what is, on the face of it, a caring expression of interest and concern is suggested by Langs (1994) in his book *Doing Supervision and Being Supervised*:

> It is essential to recognise that there are two levels of experience – two distinct dialogues – that transpire between the two parties to individual supervision. The first level of exchange is *directly stated and conscious*; it is organized around the two most basic *cognitive goals* of supervision: the education of the supervisee and…the development of the best possible therapy for the supervised patient… While this surface interchange is unfolding, there is, however, a second level of communication and experience that is also taking place. This level of interaction is *expressed indirectly and is deeply unconscious*, and it unfolds outside the awareness of the supervisory dyad. In this realm, there is a series of highly sensitive unconscious communicative exchanges between supervisor and supervisee…even as the supervisee and the supervisor are giving their full conscious attention to the material of the presented session, the deep unconscious systems of both remain focused on working over their own immediate impingements on each other within the framework of the supervisory situation. (Langs 1994, pp.2–29, his emphasis)

In distinguishing between the conscious (surface) communication and the unconscious (deep) communication Lang's exposition helps shed light on why the participant was left feeling as he did. At a conscious level the supervisor was doing and saying nothing insensitive (rather the opposite) and being kindly and concerned. Yet at a deeper, unconscious, level a communication is unfolding outside of the awareness of either party. The supervisee experiences the expression of concern as a disabling impingement ('touching an emotional well I didn't want touched'). Although supervisors are rightly criticized and found wanting at times, they walk a thin line between under and over-reaction, between showing too little concern and too much. This can also represent a common difficulty for close members of a worker's family.

Family members

Partners were sometimes helpful in acknowledging the seriousness of what had happened by the way in which they responded: 'My husband helped me by listening and by taking the next morning off work to go with me to the police.' The husband's listening is shown to be valuable here as it leads to the participant being able then to talk to the police. Taking time away from work provides recognition that something important has happened and needs to be recognized by a change in the everyday routine.

Another participant felt as if her experience had tarnished her sense of self and found that those who knew her well outside of work helped her to deal with these feelings:

> Hearing my husband's and mother's support of me was quite comforting. They said there should have been security there. They made me see it for what it really was – an assault. They helped me not to minimize it and helped me to become a victim.

Once again the sense of 'getting back' to a previous sense of self is apparent. Fear is shown to have distorted a perspective that needed to be regained ('...see it for what it really was') and the affirming, supportive response aids this process. Another participant described how her home and family life helped her to see what she encountered at work in a wider context:

> I am helped by getting back home and putting things in perspective. It reminds you that these awful things that you hear at work each day are not the general run of things. Your family helps you to realize that these

dreadful things, these wicked things that people do to themselves and others are not normal. I have three teenagers who are not angels who I persecute to be good and I talk in a general sense to my husband who thinks that social work is a terrible job.

While sharing experiences with partners and families can be helpful, this is not always the case:

Some members of staff have had to sit on their partners to stop them from wanting to come to the unit and bash the young people. I don't tell my husband anything now, because of that. One woman's husband pulled wallpaper off from a bathroom wall all night because he was so angry; and he wasn't decorating!

Family members might be perceived as well meaning but essentially unaware of how best to help workers. They could be outraged on behalf of their significant other but in a somewhat blustering, uninformed manner which leads to simplistic readings of situations such as, 'You shouldn't be asked to do that!' or, 'There's no way that you should have been left alone in there!' While such statements might contain some truth they are not often made with knowledge of the context of the work. Workers are likely to appreciate someone being on their side and feeling for them but could feel that, while their experiences have not been under-estimated, they have been misrepresented. This is not going to be helpful to them.

Recommendations for practice and training

- The considerable potential benefit of a 'community of colleagues' to support one another effectively should be recognized, allowed and encouraged by seniors in organizations as a feeling of 'belonging' and inclusion can help to counteract some of the underlying fears of separation and isolation.

- The importance of ready availability, sympathetic, initially non-evaluative, responses from those perceived of as understanding the work should be acknowledged as essential constituents of effective support.

- The profound unhelpfulness experienced when workers feel that their concerns have been dismissed, devalued or misrepresented should be appreciated.

- The characteristics of the 'ideal supervisor' should be recognized. Briefly these are 'being there' for supervisees, having time to listen without initial evaluation, understanding, acknowledging, recognizing, reflecting, validating, affirming, confirming and supporting.

- The needs of experienced workers for supervision and support should not be overlooked or minimized.

- The danger of supervision becoming a 'management preoccupation' rather than a humane, human response to those in distress should be guarded against.

- The possibility that encounters within the supervisory relationship might reflect issues arising from work with service users and/or organizational dynamics should be appreciated.

- The valuable contribution that could be made to work by internal and group supervision, in addition to one-to-one sessions, should be recognized. Conversely, so too should ways in which groups might be perceived to be 'turning on' individuals in an unhelpfully critical manner.

- The risk that supervision might be experienced as over-intrusive even when well intentioned should be acknowledged.

- The helpful and unhelpful parts played by family members in the aftermath of traumatic events should be appreciated. They can be of considerable help when listening sensitively to workers, recognizing the disabling effects of trauma and providing a sense of perspective in relation to these. They are perceived as unhelpful if they are seen as over-reacting to situations they understand little.

Chapter 8

What Helps? (2)

Management, Workplace Culture, Police Involvement, Reflection, Humour, Research

Introduction

Because managers will inevitably become involved in complaints about staff and might also act as supervisors this chapter should be read in conjunction with Chapters Six and Seven where these issues are considered. Like Chapter Seven, this chapter considers what participants found both helpful and unhelpful under the headings identified in the hope that the helpful can emerge more clearly. The chapter begins with examples of what was found to be helpful and unhelpful when participants shared fear-creating experiences with their managers. The potential help that consultants might provide to managers and organizations is acknowledged. Workplace culture is then considered. Particular ways in which fear might activate child-like responses in workers who then look to their managers to provide appropriate nurturing and controlling parental responses are discussed next by way of a transactional analysis framework. Involvement of the police at the time of or after traumatic incidents and ways in which this has been found both helpful and unhelpful are then illustrated. Helpful uses of reflection on events by discussing them with service users and by writing about them are considered as are the potential benefits of humour. The chapter concludes with a brief discussion of ways in which research itself might be therapeutic as well as illuminating and suggests some possibilities for further research into fear.

Sharing experiences with a manager

One participant spoke highly of the way in which her manager listened to her account of a situation and supported what she had done: 'My manager explored what I had done and how I felt at the end of it. He really confirmed that what I'd done was right for that particular situation.' Another said:

> I discussed a problem with my manager who was brilliant. She spoke to the staff team who had not been aware of the extent of the intimidation I was getting from two young people and the changes were amazing because all the staff backed me up with them and I got my composure back.

In these instances the manager is regarded as the sympathetic, appropriately helpful and protective parent-figure who helps the traumatized person regain a sense of perspective and balance. She provides a literal re-assurance which is of crucial importance to the worker as the experience of trauma causes her to lose her assurance, her belief and her way, at least for a while.

Sometimes management support was appreciated as it led to provision of practical resources and revised working arrangements that helped workers manage their fears better:

> Managers have acknowledged risks for us. We now have mobile phones and so do the managers in case we need to contact them. We have also agreed that two workers will go out together to undertake mental health assessments.

Once again, the crucial need to address separation anxiety is apparent as both initiatives – the provision of mobile telephones and joint working arrangements – enable workers to feel less alone and therefore more equipped to deal with their fears.

Managers were also regarded as helpful when they recognized a need in their workers and, rather than attempting to deal with it themselves, referred the worker on for specialized intervention:

> My manager referred me to a stress counsellor, somebody I respected. He was extremely helpful. He focused my mind wonderfully so that I could say I didn't want the job. He affirmed my proper professional self, my unwarped, undistorted self. He asked, 'Have you put things in writing,

what responsibility lies with you, what with others?'...a hundred different things...

Once again the distorting, warping effects of the fear experience are apparent as is the need to 'get back' to the 'proper professional self'. Although the independent counsellor provided the helpful interventions the manager is remembered as having made this possible. The managers' power to agree to additional resources, support changes in working practices and refer on for specialized help enables them to effect changes that peers cannot, however understanding and sympathetic they might be.

A social worker who had been seriously assaulted recalled his manager referring him to an independent counsellor and appreciating this:

> I saw a counsellor from Victim Support for five sessions. He provided a safe environment in which I could confront issues: the weakness, guilt and failure, all the victim stuff that happens. He had been in the social work role and had been there in a way. He helped me to understand that it's all right to be a victim. He told me that I would never be the same again. He said that there were parts of the experience I would never remember. He knew what I was talking about and could plug into it.

This worker appreciated being able to talk to someone who he perceived as being sufficiently credible to understand. Often, although not always, this entails having 'been there in a way' and being able to 'plug into it'. Managers might be too removed from the recent immediacy of practice to have such understanding, be too busy to provide such support, be insufficiently trained to do so or agree with the worker that better support is offered by a specialist from outside the organization. Referring workers on for outside help has advantages of enlisting specialist expertise when warranted and avoiding the dilemmas of managers getting to know 'too much' about their workers. However, there are also possible disadvantages as if outside agencies are listening to workers' experiences of trauma and learning lessons from these the referring organization denies itself this opportunity. Nevertheless, it is notable that some managers are remembered as being helpful for referring workers on for help rather than attempting to provide this help themselves.

Managers were thought to respond inappropriately when they failed to recognize the 'inner' impact of the experience on the worker whatever the 'outer' reality. One participant was threatened with violence from a service user that did not materialize. Because 'nothing (actually) happened' her supervisor took the view that no particular hardship had been suffered but the participant felt differently saying, 'The disbelief of others was unhelpful. What *might* happen was as important as what *did* happen.' This brief encapsulation, once again, is testament to the power of the imagination in bringing fearful possibilities to life in the mind even when they do not exist in the outer 'real' world. It is crucial to recognize the power of this process as people can die as a result of what they fear, even when what they fear does not materialize (see Chapter Two).

Just as individual workers can benefit from supervision, organizations can also be enriched by their work being inspected by and discussed with a consultant from outside the organization (Cooklin 1999; Menzies-Lyth 1992; Obholzer and Roberts 1994). Not being party to organizational history, culture, written and unwritten rules, dominant and subservient factions the consultant can take a more detached view of what seems apparent and suggest what strategies and defensive manoeuvres are employed by the organization to guard against anxiety. In this role, however, the consultant is likely to be perceived with ambivalence, simultaneously welcomed and feared:

> The consultant who undertakes to explore the nature of the underlying difficulty is likely to be seen as an object of both hope and fear. The conscious hope is that the problem will be brought to the surface, but at the same time, unconsciously, this is the very thing that institutions fear. (Halton 1994, p.12)

This quotation illustrates the ambivalent and, at times, paradoxical nature of fear and its functioning. The organization makes use of defences to guard against what it fears. At least part of the response to these fears being uncovered is further fear. The fears therefore grow, inter-twine and multiply, feeding on one another.

Ward and McMahon (1998, p.63) suggest that in an ideal setting the benefits of individual and group supervision, both made more beneficial by effective consultancy, will all work together for the combined benefit of the individual and organization:

> ...people need regular and reliable opportunities first to reflect in supervision upon their work; second to communicate with each other in staff meetings about these thoughts and feelings and third, to gauge their own

feelings against external reality through external management or consultation. The outcome of all this support and management should be that people are enabled to be 'real' and present at work in a very direct and personal way, not only as individuals but also as a team.

The extent to which these elements will be able to work together for the common good will be determined primarily by the prevalent workplace culture.

Workplace culture: the parent and the child

Workplace culture can be defined broadly as 'the way things are done around here' (Coulshed and Mullender 2001, p.50) or as the sum of the norms, beliefs, values and metaphors prevalent in an organization at a point in time (Gorman 1998, p.115). All workplaces have cultures and these will prove more influential in determining what work gets done and how than any number of written policies and procedures however well worded or appropriate these might be.

Many people will spend a substantial part of their lives at work so the working environment assumes a great importance for them. Despite the fact that perceived low pay appears to feature frequently as a source of discontent several research studies have shown that pay is relatively low down the list of priorities when people are asked what is of most importance to them in their working lives. Handy (1999, p.28) quotes one study which revealed what people most wanted from their work. The most mentioned attributes were:

- personal freedom
- respect of colleagues
- learning something new
- challenge
- completing a project
- helping other people.

Money came twenty-fourth on this list.

Thompson (1995, p.52) cites another study which found that people wanted:

- personal freedom

- increased responsibility
- praise from superiors
- respect from work colleagues.

'Making money' was ranked twenty-eighth in order of importance.

People are therefore likely to choose work that they think will satisfy their deeper psychological needs as far as they are able. Because of this they enter into a 'psychological contract' (Handy 1999, p.36) which might be quite different from, and is certainly more substantial than, the contract that they actually sign. Psychological contracts are frequently unspoken and this secrecy makes their influence all the more subtle. Most people have encountered situations in the workplace when what is happening between people seems to be out of all proportion to what has ostensibly provoked an incident. There seems much more at stake for the people concerned than the apparently relatively trivial incident that has triggered an argument. Often there is, but the protagonists will rarely admit as much. It is also possible that they are not fully aware of the extent to which their secret psychological contract has been breached by others who are, themselves, frequently ignorant of the extent of the damage they have unwittingly caused. At such times logic appears to be forgotten and powerful emotions hold sway. As Handy (1999, p.99) comments, '…human beings are not always logical, they are psychological, they think with their feelings as much as their brains'.

It is apparent from the examples already provided how psychologically de-stabilizing an experience of fear can be for health and social care workers. To experience fear is typically to revert to a child-like state and, as such, to then look around for strong, protective, parental figures who can help. The ego states of parent, adult and child described and employed by transactional analysis (Berne 1975; Stewart and Joines 2002) offer a helpful additional model to that of attachment theory which has previously been referred to in this book. People of all ages are capable of parent, adult and/or child ego state responses to situations.

When operating primarily in a child ego state a person will be demonstrating the behaviours, thoughts and feelings which are replayed from their own childhood. The child ego state is divided into the adapted child, who conforms to rules and societal demands, and the free child who expresses feelings and wants without censoring and without reference to the rules and societal demands which constrain the adapted child. The parent ego state can be subdivided into the controlling parent who controls, directs and criticizes and the nurturing parent who nurtures, cares and helps.

Fearful workers will often experience a regression to a child ego state and will therefore (consciously or unconsciously) turn to those in authority to play the role of parents and help them out. Workers are therefore likely to treat their managers and supervisors as they treated previous authority figures encountered throughout their upbringing. It is often this re-playing of past conflicts (and/or triumphs) that are liable to confuse protagonists as ghosts from the past intrude upon fears experienced in the present and exert their influence in unseen and unrecognized ways. Managers and supervisors might receive all manner of inappropriate projections from workers who respond to them in their parental roles.

Fear-provoking and traumatic situations are liable also to trigger the manager's child ego state as she too might become frightened of threatening possibilities. She, in turn, will look to her manager to act as a good parent looking after her and hope for a sympathetic strong container rather than a critical, rigid, condemner. As well as being divided into controlling or nurturing the parent ego state is subdivided further still as these two parent ego states both have positive and negative functions. A positive controlling parent is genuinely concerned with protecting and promoting the wellbeing of the child while the negative controlling parent will put down and discount. Positive nurturing parenting provides caring from a starting point of genuine regard for the person helped while the negatively nurturing parent is ostensibly helpful and caring while actually being undermining and de-skilling. Parents saying, 'Here, let me do that for you', taking a difficult task away from a child and thus denying her the opportunity of mastery under the guise of helping, and the 'smother-mother' are examples of negative nurturing parents.

In transactional analysis terms a positive workplace culture is one which allows workers, temporarily regressed to child ego states, to experience fears and be responded to by way of parental ego states that combine appropriate measures of control (protection) and nurture (care). Another useful term from transactional analysis is the 'stroke' which means a unit of recognition. We all need positive strokes from others if we are to flourish and these positive strokes are what most people want from their managers, supervisors and colleagues in the work environment. Too often managers seem to be in conflict with and in opposition to those they manage so that workers fear negative parenting responses should they expose the vulnerability that has been opened by their fears. Recognizing the potential weakness of even the strongest workers and employing the language of transactional analysis, Handy (1999, p.100) comments, 'The truth is that we are all insecure at heart and we all respond positively to being psychologically stroked. And stroking lasts longer than striking.'

Workers will not be able to share and move on from their fears in workplace cultures which primarily employ striking rather than stroking. All of us, from most junior to most senior workers, are liable to be strongly affected by experiences of fear and in that we share a common humanity whatever our status in the organization. 'Us and them' positions adopted by workers and managers are therefore not helpful in this respect. Covey's advice that organizations should look for 'win/win or no deal' solutions in the workplace and that *seeking first to understand, then to be understood* is the 'single most important principle in the field of interpersonal relations' (Covey 1992, p.237) could usefully be heeded by those wanting to establish workplace cultures conducive to positive working.

In addition to commenting upon the workplace culture prevalent in their own organization workers often mentioned the police (in transactional analysis terms the ultimate parents!) when talking of their experiences of fear. Examples of police involvement are now considered.

Police involvement

Police involvement was frequently mentioned in social work participants' accounts of stress and fear. Sometimes, in the heat of a crisis, a response from the police was requested to deal with the incident. On other occasions participants described reporting an incident to the police once the crisis had passed. Like most responses to fear-provoking incidents the police were remembered as being both helpful and unhelpful. However, they were more often thought to be helpful, usually providing timely and effective assistance and containment when the crisis was at its height. A number of participants found a catharsis in making a statement to the police. Telling the story of what had happened in meticulous detail to a careful listener afforded benefits which feature as part of some psychological de-briefing (Parkinson 1993) processes when these are conducted appropriately and well.

While timely and effective responses from the police were much appreciated delays and confusion, understandably, were not. Two home carers were assaulted by a man who had been drunk and recalled:

> The police were delayed for half an hour getting there and when they did arrive they went to the house of the dying lady we'd just put to bed and got her out of bed again to answer the door. Having been mucked around by the police I was told to come into reception to give a statement. Having got there, I was told to go home and wait for someone to visit. I received no sympathy at all.

Whereas making a statement to the police could be a helpful and cathartic way of constructing memory and meanings, it was not always found to be helpful, particularly if the process was fragmented:

> Not finishing my statement with the police immediately after the incident was unhelpful. I had to wait until the following night when they came to see me at home to do this. It would be better to do it all in one go. It brought everything back in an unhelpful way going through it all in minute detail again.

Although talking about fears to an appropriately concerned and trusted other can be helpful this quotation shows how such talking might be experienced as essentially unhelpful. Reflecting upon experiences was cited as an additional help to workers attempting to deal with fear-provoking experiences.

Reflection

One residential social worker was experiencing considerable and protracted difficulties with two young people in her care and was thinking about this. She recalls:

> I was walking to school with another young person who didn't have a problem with me and with whom I had a good relationship and she said, 'The way those kids treat you is totally out of order.' At that point I had lost faith in all young people, they were all 'morons' and 'idiots'. When she had gone I thought, 'Thank you! Bless you! I'll do anything for you now.' She showed me that she didn't have a problem with me, it's them

who had the problem and I should stop taking it so personally. I wrote on her card when she left, 'Thank you for restoring my faith in young people again.'

The young person's comments in the context of the worker's reflection had a powerful and healing effect. It is heartening to recognize that faith can be restored, as well as lost, as a result of contact with service users.

Reflecting on events by way of writing about them was valued by several participants. One social worker wrote up a visit during which she thought she might have been assaulted just prior to going on holiday and reflected, 'In hindsight writing it down was helpful, although at the time it did not seem helpful – just a chore.' The very process of writing moves material from inside the person to outside and thus gives it more of an 'objectivity' that can be shared with appropriate others. It is a way of 'bearing witness' or 'giving testimony' to the experience and some of its effects (Raphael 1990). Having written the account shredding rough notes before going home can give a sense of release and satisfaction. One social worker saw writing as an essential step in the processing of difficult experiences:

> I would drive my car and stop and write up these visits at once and it seems as if some of it leaves your head and goes down on the page as you are writing. I would not have got a reasonable night's sleep if I had not written it down; it would be jangling around my head.

Sometimes the writing undertaken could form part of an official record: case notes, a court report or a letter. On other occasions the writing might be more creative and struggles with fear symbolized by way of images and metaphor in a reflective journal (Bolton 1999; Cameron 1995; Ferrucci 1995). Such forms of creative writing can help individuals come to understand their traumatized and care-taking selves better, particularly when these are considered from multiple points of view (Bell and Magrs 2001).

Humour

Humour is well known to function as a coping mechanism for people dealing with stressful situations. It provides a means of responding to and attempting to cope with traumatic material and is often of a 'gallows' nature (Berne 1975; Kuhlman 1988; Sullivan 2000) which provides grim recognition of unpleasant possibilities and realities. One participant described the benefits of laughter and humour as follows:

> Laughter is one of the best lifters, being flippant. Although it's a very serious thing. I've got to lighten it. A sense of humour is great. It helps me get back to myself.

Once again the desire to 'get back' to a pre-traumatized state is apparent. Another participant also described humour as something that lightened a load:

> You need to lighten the way you feel physically. You feel heavy, weighed down with it, and someone making a joke of it lightens it.

Jeffers (1991, p.37) also advocates the advantages of lightness, suggesting that there is great value in not taking even the most important things too seriously: 'Angels fly because they take themselves lightly.' An advantage of humour, like writing, is that it depends essentially on seeing something from another point of view. If people have a range of possible perspectives they have options and options entail choices. People could choose therefore to be less adversely affected by fear-creating experiences than would be the case if they thought themselves to be bound so closely to one way of seeing the incident that they could not escape it.

Humour can be a wonderful healing release in fraught circumstances when used by the right person in the right way at the right time. Conversely, failed attempts at humour can be remembered as crassly insensitive and appallingly inappropriate. In this respect humour was remembered by participants as being both helpful and unhelpful as a response to fear as were most responses.

Research: talking about fears – helpful or unhelpful?

Fears are often coped with by denial. To some extent this is necessary and essential to good mental health. If any one of us opened ourselves up to the full extent of each of our fears we would not be able to function. On the other hand, unless we talk about some of our fears to some extent we deny ourselves the opportunity to confront, challenge and overcome these fears and thus lead fuller and richer lives. It is a question of balance (see Afterword).

One worker said, 'When talking you re-live it in a certain way, not in such detail as when you were there, but you do re-live it, and each time you tell it, it gets less.' This is the argument in favour of giving fear words, that it diminishes with repeated telling. It is an underpinning principle of much counselling and psychotherapy. Conversely, a different worker expressed a fear that if she started crying about her fears she would be unable to stop; like the unwitting sorcerer's apprentice, she might set a process in motion she was unable to control subsequently:

> It's like having little shelves in the back of your brain to stack things – sad things, frightening things. You're frightened if you talk about it too much that it would get too big to get back on the shelf.

These two points of view show how talking about fears could be either helpful, or unhelpful. Some participants grew as people as a result of their fear-provoking experience and, although they would not have chosen it, thought they had benefited from the experience. Others continued to have nightmares about it and wished it had never happened.

Several participants in the research studies said that they found talking about their experiences by way of the research interview was helpful to them. This was because the interview cleared a time and space in a busy work schedule to reflect upon and share what they had experienced in the hope of understanding it better. It also provided an opportunity for seeing things differently, perhaps entailing use of humour. It seemed important that the researcher's role combined:

- some, although not necessarily detailed, knowledge of participants' work
- a genuine interest in the participant's story, recognizing they were 'the expert'
- a non-evaluative role in relation to the participant's performance.

Writing further on people's secret psychological contracts (see above) Handy (1999, p.42) comments:

> All work, after all, is a partnership of some kind. The secret contract made less secret acknowledges this fact, and, by bringing it out into the open, makes it more negotiable. Left secret, people can feel exploited, manipu-

lated or ignored and their bosses can become, in their turn, disappointed, angry or disillusioned.

The contention here is that there are advantages in appropriately bringing to light strong influences on the motivation to work that were hidden previously. In many ways this is what the research described in this book is attempting to do. The essential belief is that there is a benefit in 'naming' powerful processes (Hughes and Pengelly 1998, p.152) and naming often requires that things are articulated before they can be understood. In hoping to begin this articulation/recognition/understanding process with regard to experiences of fear and ways in which these might affect workers in health and social care work I acknowledge that there is much more that could be done. My hope has been to sketch a general picture and there are many specific areas and points of detail that could be studied further to benefit. In particular, future research could usefully be conducted into:

- differences between fears of workers of different genders and ages
- the influence of race, culture and sexuality on fears
- fears arising from work in different geographical locations
- differences between fears of front-line workers and managers/supervisors
- workplace cultures that have been successful in helping workers deal with fears
- training that enables workers to access helpful responses when traumatized.

Recommendations for practice and training

- Managers should be aware of how helpful they can be to workers affected by fear-provoking experiences by listening to them, seeing events from their perspective and providing practical assistance when appropriate.
- Managers should also appreciate that they can sometimes help more not by listening themselves but by referring workers on to other sources of help.

- The potential help that consultants can give to managers should be recognized.

- The fact that experiences of fear will trigger child-like responses in workers and their managers alike should be acknowledged. This raises questions as to what an appropriate 'parental' response should be.

- The importance of 'stroking' rather than 'striking' should be recognized and absorbed into workplace cultures.

- The fact that money features relatively low down the list of what people most want from their working environment should be thoughtfully considered.

- The greater importance of the (secret) psychological contract over the (actual) signed contract should be appreciated.

- Looking for win/win solutions and seeking first to understand others before being understood oneself should be the norm.

- Policies should be in place which clearly specify when workers should involve the police at the time of, and after, traumatic events.

- Time should be made available for workers to reflect on fear-provoking events, alone, perhaps by way of writing, and with service users.

- Research should be recognized as being of potential therapeutic as well as illuminating value as it helps to bring to light and *name* important underlying aspects of people in the work setting. It should also be acknowledged, however, that some people will prefer to try to cope with their experiences of fear by not thinking or talking about them and this choice should be respected.

Afterword

The Gift of Fear

Fear: gift or curse?

Fear has so many unpleasant and negative aspects that it is unsurprising that people do not often welcome or enjoy it. Although, as many of the stories gathered in this book attest, experiences of fear can be extremely difficult to live with and rise above, there is another aspect of fear which enriches and teaches. The person who had no concept of fear would soon be seriously injured or killed and to be beyond fear could contribute to the kind of psychotic, satanic omnipotence portrayed by Shakespeare [1606] (1965) in the character of Macbeth:

> O, full of scorpions is my mind...
> Come seeling night, Scarf up the tender eye of pitiful day;
> And with thy bloody and invisible hand
> Cancel and tear to pieces that great bond which keeps me pale!
> Light thickens; and the crow makes wing to th' rooky wood:
> Good things of day begin to droop and drowse;
> While night's black agents to their preys do rouse.
>
> (Act III, Scene ii)

Tenderness and the inhibition against breaking social convention bred of fear, which would usually prevent people from harming or killing others, are cancelled and torn to pieces as Macbeth justifies his inexorable advance into more and more bloodshed. Earlier on in the play he is shown to be afraid of the dagger he hallucinates and of Banquo's ghost at his banquet.

Towards the end of the play he reflects on this loss of his capacity to feel fear almost as a loss of innocence:

> I have almost forgot the taste of fears:
> The time has been, my sense would have cool'd to hear a night-shriek;
> And my fell of hair would at a dismal treatise rouse and stir as life were in't:
> I have supt full with horrors; Direness, familiar to my slaughterous thoughts,
> Cannot once start me.

(Act V, Scene v)

Macbeth recalls an earlier time when he would have felt a cold shiver of fear, hearing an owl shriek at night and when his hairs would stand up on hearing a horror story but he now feels beyond any such response; his sensibility to fear blunted as he has 'supt full with horrors'. In this respect Shakespeare is portraying fear as a useful inhibitor of people's more violent potential which, if ignored or superseded, could have fatal consequences.

The psychoanalyst W.R. Bion (1994, p.292) acknowledges fear as potential curse or gift. He writes of, 'thalmic fear – the fear which is so powerful that it makes thinking impossible'. Usually not being able to think puts the individual at a disadvantage as all that he knows deserts him or is inaccessible to him. This is the kind of fear that leaves the rabbit paralysed in the car headlights, unable to move and in danger of being killed. Even so, this fear has its roots in preservation of life as if an animal thought it heard a predator in the bushes, to freeze or 'play dead' might be the most effective way of ensuring survival as it then makes no sound thus helping avoid detection or further interest.

Elsewhere Bion (1990, p.5) claims that experiencing fear contributes to the best work possible between helper and helped (in this case psychoanalyst and patient):

> Anyone who is going to see a patient tomorrow should, at some point, experience fear. In every consulting room there ought to be two rather frightened people: the patient and the psychoanalyst. If they are not, one wonders why they are bothering to find out what everyone knows.

Here Bion acknowledges that fear sharpens receptivity, hones attention and does not allow a comfortable, and perhaps complacent, feeling that the helper has 'heard it all before' or knows what they are dealing with without making allowance for the uniquely subjective perspective of each individual on different occasions. People are more careful when they are fearful and thus likely to attend more appropriately to their own personal safety needs; 'Best safety lies in fear' (Shakespeare [1604] 1986: *Hamlet* Act I, Scene iii). A drawback of works with titles like, 'Living without fear' and 'Driving fear out of the workplace' is that these do not acknowledge the potential advantages of getting to know and understand how fear might be an ally – indeed one of the most valuable we have.

De Becker (1997, p.11) suggests, 'Since fear is so central to our experience, understanding when it is a gift – and when a curse – is well worth the effort.' Cohen (2003) distinguishes between valuable, useful fears and unproductive fears, between survival fear and unnecessary fear. He suggests (2003, p.79), 'There is only one fear we all need – the instinctive, primal fear that is meant to protect us from harm or life-threatening situations.' People mis-apply this 'primal' fear to situations which do not warrant it and thereby live unnecessarily diminished and restricted lives. The great difficulty in understanding and befriending fear effectively is that it is a multi-faceted, multi-layered emotion comprised of irrational and rational elements. No sooner do we think we have understood it to some extent than it reveals another level and a different aspect. We are tantalized with the prospect of an impossible quest, suspecting that, ultimately, real fear is unknowable. As Kafka (quoted in Beradt 1985, p.65) puts it, 'Ah yes, but that is not the real fear. The real fear is fear of what lies beneath the surface of things, and this fear will not be dispelled.'

Despite these difficulties it is worth getting to know fear better as our most valuable achievements often emerge from the shadows of our greatest fears. Acknowledging and responding to one's fears can have a transforming effect as Steven Spielberg, the film director, explains:

> I used to fear going to school. I used to fear getting pounded by the bigger kids. I used to fear being humiliated on the baseball field. I used to fear having my heart broken by gorgeous babes who wouldn't date me. I used to fear everything... I used to terrorize audiences so that I could have some control over what scared me. In *Poltergeist*, I took all my fears of the unknown and put them in one film to exorcise them. It was like teasing my kid sister – except more profitable... (Spielberg 1998)

Few workers in health and social care settings are going to experience success on the scale of Steven Spielberg or the film director Alfred Hitchcock or author Stephen King who have moulded their fascination with fear into their life's work. Even so, the potential benefits of appropriately addressing and transforming fears are available to most. If we are going to unwrap and benefit from the gift of fear we need to be able to talk about it.

Whereof we cannot speak…

Although there can be disadvantages in talking about fears (see Chapter Eight) and some people might be concerned that attempting to do so could result in more harm than good, this book rests on the premise that it is usually good to talk. That fears are often better (appropriately) out than in. In their work highlighting difficulties experienced by African Caribbean users of health and social care services the Sainsbury Centre (2002) draw attention to how not being able to talk about these difficulties contributes to self-perpetuating 'circles of fear' which, in turn, make it more difficult for people to express their fears.

Drawing attention to the fact that social workers in Northern Ireland often respond to 'the troubles' by not talking about them, Campbell and Healey (1999, p.396) cite the '…popular Northern Irish maxim: "whatever you say, you say nothing"' as a possible reason for this. They make the point that fearful possibilities are often responded to with a silence which inhibits the possibility of greater understanding. In their paper entitled '"Whatever you say, say something": the education, training and practice of mental health social workers in Northern Ireland' they suggest that people give their fears words as without a willingness to examine and share them they cannot be thought of and learned from.

Finding an appropriate language that can be shared is the most valuable starting point. If we cannot do this we are condemned to the silence of incomprehension. As Wittgenstein (1961, p.74) puts it, 'Whereof we cannot speak, thereof we must pass over in silence.'

Fear can save life or take life. It is in our interests to become more familiar with it so that we can harness its life-enhancing and life-preserving capacities and reduce its potentially fatal consequences. We can be helped in this task by considering a contribution to the debate from Aristotle (1981).

Fearing the right thing to the right extent at the right time in the right way

Aristotle advocated that people saw both good and bad as inherent in the same thing and that an appropriate sense of balance and proportion was needed to hold a necessary tension. He wrote:

> It is possible to fear [some] things too much or too little, and also to fear what is not fearful as it were. One kind of error is to be afraid of the wrong thing, another to be afraid in the wrong way, and another at the wrong time... (Aristotle 1981, p.128)

Aristotle is therefore claiming that the person who gets the balance right is he who discovers how to fear the right thing to the right extent, at the right time, in the right way. A person who dies of a heart attack brought on by the mistaken belief that a stick is a poisonous snake has unnecessarily feared the wrong thing to the wrong extent, at the wrong time in the wrong way. Another, who is convicted of a crime he thought would avoid detection, has not feared sufficiently the right thing, to the right extent, at the right time, in the right way.

One famous example of a person fearing the wrong thing in the wrong way concerns the ballerina Isodora Duncan who died from strangulation when her long scarf was caught in a wheel of her open-topped sports car (Doctor and Kahn 1989). Duncan would only travel in open-topped cars as her sons had drowned in a closed-top car. Influenced by her fear, she avoiding travelling in closed-top cars thinking this would keep her alive. Ironically, it was this very act that brought about her death as her scarf would almost certainly not have become caught in the same way had she been travelling in a closed-top car.

Fearing the wrong thing to the wrong extent also has application to groups and societies as well as individuals. In *Pure Madness: How Fear Drives the Mental Health System*, Laurence (2003) analyses a relatively small number of high-profile and much-reported killings by people suffering mental illness. He shows how these killings have evoked a government response including proposals of severely restrictive legislation in an attempt to prevent such killings from happening in future. The popularly accepted belief appears to be that society is becoming more and more dangerous as people are increasingly at risk of random killings by complete strangers suffering mental illness. Controlling legislation is thought necessary to stem this tide. At the time of writing the Mental Health Act 1983 is being considered for revision. Opponents of the new proposals claim that they are more aimed at social order than mental health and more concerned with reducing risk than providing treatment and care.

Laurence (2003) extensively researched mental health provision and practices and writes:

> What I found was a service driven by fear in which the priority is risk reduction through containment – by physical or chemical means… It was not always like this. Professionals say that it is only in the last five years that the pressure from a government and public averse to risk and bent on pinning blame when things go wrong has produced a culture of containment in the mental health service seen in rising detention, increasing use of medication, locked wards and growing dissatisfaction among the users of the services. (Laurence 2003, p.xix)

What is the evidence that mentally ill people are potentially more dangerous at this point in time and therefore need greater social confinement than ever before? Laurence doesn't find any:

> Yet figures show there has been no increase in killings by people with a mental illness in the forty years during which the mental hospitals have been emptying. The argument that community care policy has increased risks to the public cannot be sustained. Fewer than one in ten murders is committed by someone with a mental disorder and over the last four decades they have accounted for a diminishing proportion of all homicides as the overall murder rate has risen. (Laurence 2003, p.xviii)

Laurence demonstrates that while the number of murders committed by people suffering mental illness has remained fairly constant over the past forty years the number committed by people without mental illness has risen. Therefore the proportion of murders by mentally ill people has actually fallen over this time. Laurence concludes that the motivation for more controlling legislation does not stem from evidence of increased danger to the general public from those suffering mental illness but from generally less permissive and more fearful attitudes. While public fears focus on 'stranger danger' and the mad axe-man on the loose people are more likely to be killed by a heavy drinker, especially one who drives. Mentally ill people are more likely to be murdered than to murder, being six times more likely to die by homicide than the general population

(Laurence 2003, p.66). In Aristotle's terms the proposed new legislation shows a fear of the wrong thing, in the wrong way at the wrong time.

This book constitutes an attempt to understand fears of health and social care workers better by reporting, thinking about and analysing their accounts of fearful experiences. It rests on the belief that an enhanced understanding of fear will help these workers carry out their tasks more efficiently and safely. Fear can be a curse or a gift. Individuals will determine which of these it is to some extent by how they perceive, think about and share the fear stimulus. Time spent getting to know and make friends with fear is time well spent. Although a tyrannical master it is a wonderful servant. If we can get the balance right and know how to fear the right thing to the right extent, at the right time, in the right way we will have learned a most valuable lesson. In the words of Kierkegaard [1844] (1944, p.139):

> He therefore who has learned rightly to be in dread has learned the most important thing.

References

American Psychiatric Association (1994) *Diagnostic and Statistical Manual of Mental Disorders (Fourth Edition)*. Washington DC: American Psychiatric Association.

Aristotle (1981) *Ethics*. Harmondsworth: Penguin.

Balloch, S., Pahl, J. and McLean, J. (1998) 'Working in the social services: job satisfaction, stress and violence.' *British Journal of Social Work 28*, 329–350.

Barker, C.M. [1923] (1986) *Flower Fairies of the Summer*. London: Blackie.

Bell, J. and Magrs, P. (2001) *The Creative Writing Coursebook*. London: Macmillan.

Beradt, C. (1985) *The Third Reich of Dreams: the Nightmares of a Nation 1933–1939*. Wellingborough: The Aquarian Press.

Berger, J. (1972) *Ways of Seeing*. London: Penguin.

Berne, E. (1975) *What do you Say After you Say Hello?* London: Corgi.

Bettelheim, B. (1979) *The Uses of Enchantment. The Meaning and Importance of Fairy Tales*. London: Penguin.

Bibby, P. (1994) *Personal Safety for Social Workers*. London: Arena.

Binder, R. (1991) 'Women clinicians and patient assaults.' *Bulletin of American Academic Psychiatry and Law 19*, 3, 291–296.

Bion, W.R. (1990) *Brazilian Lectures*. London: Karnac.

Bion, W.R. (1994) *Clinical Seminars and Other Works*. London: Karnac.

Bolton, G. (1999) *The Therapeutic Potential of Creative Writing: Writing Myself*. London: Jessica Kingsley Publishers.

Botting, F. (1996) *Gothic*. London: Routledge.

Bowlby, J. (1973) *Separation, Anxiety and Anger: Volume Two of Attachment and Loss*. London: Hogarth Press.

Bowlby, J. (1988) *A Secure Base: Clinical Applications of Attachment Theory*. London: Routledge.

Braithwaite, R. (2001) *Managing Aggression*. London: Routledge.

Buyssen, H. (1996) *Traumatic Experiences of Nurses: When Your Profession Becomes a Nightmare*. London: Jessica Kingsley Publishers.

Cairns, K. (1999) *Surviving Paedophilia: Traumatic Stress after Organised and Network Child Sexual Abuse*. Staffordshire: Trentham.

Cameron. J. (1995) *The Artist's Way*. London: Pan Macmillan.

Campbell, J. and Healey, A. (1999) '"Whatever you say, say something": the education, training and practice of mental health social workers in Northern Ireland.' *Social Work Education 18*, 4, 389–400.

Carroll, N. (1990) *The Philosophy of Horror, or, Paradoxes of the Heart*. London: Routledge.

Casement, P. (1985) *On Learning from the Patient*. London: Routledge.

Chapman, T. (1992) 'Who is afraid? Managing anxieties in a youth club.' In E. Noonan and L. Spurling (eds) *The Making of a Counsellor*. London: Routledge.

Clifton, J. and Serdar, H. (2003) *Bully Off! Recognising and Tackling Workplace Bullying.* Lyme Regis: Russell House.

Cohen, P. (2003) *Fear Busting: A Proven Plan to Beat Fear and Change Your Life.* London: Element.

Coleridge, S.T. [1802] (1987) *Selected Poems.* Edited by J. Reeve. London: Heinemann.

Conan Doyle, A. [1902] (1996) *The Hound of the Baskervilles.* Harmondsworth: Penguin.

Cook, K. and Kelly, L. (1997) 'The abduction of credibility. A reply to John Paley.' *British Journal of Social Work 27,* 1, 71–84.

Cooklin, A. (ed) (1999) *Changing Organizations: Clinicians as Agents of Change.* London: Karnac.

Cooper, A. (2000) 'The state of mind we're in.' *Soundings 3,* 1, 118–138.

Coulshed, V. and Mullender, A. (2001) *Management in Social Work (Second Edition).* Hampshire: Palgrave.

Covey, S. (1992) *The Seven Habits of Highly Effective People.* London: Simon and Schuster.

Daley, T. (ed) (1984) *Art as Therapy: An Introduction to the Use of Art as a Therapeutic Technique.* London: Tavistock.

Davies, R. (ed) (1998) *Stress in Social Work.* London: Jessica Kingsley Publishers.

De Becker, G. (1997) *The Gift of Fear: Survival Signals that Protect us from Violence.* London: Bloomsbury.

Department of Health (1991) *Child Abuse: A Study of Inquiry Reports 1980–1989.* London: HMSO.

Department of Health (1995) *Child Protection: Messages from Research.* London: HMSO.

Department of Health (2000) *Framework for the Assessment of Children in Need and their Families.* London: HMSO.

Department of Health (2002) *Learning from Past Experience: A Review of Serious Case Reviews.* London: HMSO.

Dockar-Drysdale, B. (1990) *The Provision of Primary Experience: Winnicottian Work with Children and Adolescents.* London: Free Association Books.

Doctor, R. and Kahn, A. (1989) *The Encyclopedia of Phobias, Fears and Anxieties.* Oxford: Facts on File.

Ekman, P. (2003) *Emotions Revealed: Understanding Faces and Feelings.* London: Weidenfeld and Nicolson.

Erikson, E. [1951] (1977) *Childhood and Society.* London: Triad/Granada.

Ferrucci, P. (1995) *What We May Be: The Vision and Techniques of Psychosynthesis.* London: Thorsons.

Fordham, F. (1966) *An Introduction to Jung's Psychology.* London: Penguin.

Freud, S. (1953) *Three Essays on the Theory of Sexuality (Standard Edition Vol VII).* London: Hogarth Press.

Freud, S. (1955a) *Beyond the Pleasure Principle (Standard Edition Vol XVIII).* London: Hogarth Press.

Freud, S. (1955b) *Group Psychology and the Analysis of the Ego (Standard Edition Vol XVIII).* London: Hogarth Press.

Freud, S. (1955c) *The Uncanny (Standard Edition Vol XVII).* London: Hogarth Press.

Freud, S. (1959) *Inhibitions, Symptoms and Anxiety (Standard Edition Vol XX).* London: Hogarth Press.

Freud, S. (1961) *Humour (Standard Edition Vol XXI).* London: Hogarth Press.

Froggett, L. (2000) 'Staff supervision and dependency culture: a case study.' *Journal of Social Work Practice 14*, 1, 27–35.

Frosh, S. (1987) 'Facing disclosure: common anxieties when interviewing sexually abused children.' *Practice 1*, 2, 129–136.

Goffman, E. [1959] (1978) *The Presentation of Self in Everyday Life*. Harmondsworth: Penguin.

Gordon, P. (1996) 'A fear of difference? Some reservations about intercultural therapy and counselling.' *Psychodynamic Counselling 2*, 2, 195–208.

Gorman, P. (1998) *Managing Multi-Disciplinary Teams in the NHS*. London: Kogan Page.

Grant, S. (2003) 'Suspended doctors' suicide fear.' *Health Service Journal*. 11 September, p.7.

Halton, W. (1994) 'Some unconscious aspects of organisational life: contributions from psychoanalysis.' In A. Obholzer and V. Roberts (eds) *The Unconscious at Work: Individual and Organisational Stress in the Human Services*. London: Routledge.

Handy, C. (1999) *Inside Organizations: Twenty-one Ideas for Managers*. London: Penguin.

Hawkins, P. and Shohet, R. (1990) *Supervision in the Helping Professions*. Milton Keynes: Open University Press.

Hawthorne, N. [1850] (1986) *The Scarlet Letter and Selected Tales*. London: Penguin.

Herman, J. (2001) *Trauma and Recovery: From Domestic Abuse to Political Terror*. London: Pandora.

Hughes, L. and Pengelly, P. (1998) *Staff Supervision in a Turbulent Environment: Managing Process and Task in Front-line Services*. London: Jessica Kingsley Publishers.

Hunt, G. (1995) *Whistleblowing in the Health Service: Accountability, Law and Professional Practice*. London: Edward Arnold.

Hunt, G. (1998) *Whistleblowing in the Social Services: Public Accountability and Professional Practice*. London: Edward Arnold.

Jacobs, M. (1988) *Psychodynamic Counselling in Action*. London: Sage.

Jeffers, S. (1991) *Feel the Fear and do it Anyway*. London: Arrow.

Jennings, S. (ed) (1997) *Dramatherapy: Theory and Practice, Volume 3*. London: Routledge.

Jennings, S. and Minde, A. (1993) *Art Therapy and Drama Therapy: Masks of the Soul*. London: Routledge.

Jung, C. (1978) *Man and his Symbols*. London: Picador.

Kafka, F. [1925] (1978) *The Trial*. Harmondsworth: Penguin.

Kierkegaard, S. [1844] (1944) *The Concept of Dread*. Oxford University Press.

Klein, M. [1932] (1975) *The Psycho-Analysis of Children*. London: Hogarth Press.

Klein, M. (1988) *Envy and Gratitude and Other Works 1946–1963*. London: Virago.

Kuhlman, T. (1988) 'Gallows humour for a scaffold setting: managing aggressive patients on a maximum-security forensic unit.' *Hospital and Community Psychiatry 39*, 10, 1085–1090.

Laming, H. (2003) *The Victoria Climbié Inquiry*. Norwich: HMSO.

Langs, R. (1994) *Doing Supervision and Being Supervised*. London: Karnac.

Laurence, J. (2003) *Pure Madness: How Fear Drives the Mental Health System*. London: Routledge.

LeDoux, J. (1998) *The Emotional Brain*. London: Orion.

Levey, S. and Howells, K. (1995) 'Dangerousness, unpredictability and the fear of people with schizophrenia.' *Journal of Forensic Psychiatry 6*, 1, 19–39.

London Borough of Brent (1985) *The Report of the Panel of Inquiry into the Circumstances Surrounding the Death of Jasmine Beckford*. London: Kingswood.

Magilner, M. (1996) 'Absolutely fatal. The fear of death and the mid-life crisis.' *Psychodynamic Counselling 2*, 2, 257–262.

Mann, A. (1992) 'Debt counselling.' In E. Noonan and L. Spurling (eds) *The Making of a Counsellor*. London: Routledge.

Marijana, S. (1996) 'When fear blinds the mind's eye.' *Group Analysis 29*, 4, 527–534.

Marks, I. (1980) *Living with Fear: Understanding and Coping with Anxiety*. London: McGraw-Hill.

Martin, P. (1997) *The Sickening Mind: Brain Behaviour, Immunity and Disease*. London: HarperCollins.

Mattingly, M. (1981) 'Occupational stress for group care personnel.' In F. Ainsworth and L. Fulcher (eds) *Group Care for Children: Concept and Issues*. London: Tavistock.

Mattinson, J. (1975) *The Reflection Process in Casework Supervision*. London: The Institute of Marital Studies.

May, R. (1991) *The Cry for Myth*. London: Souvenir Press.

Menzies-Lyth, I. (1992) *Containing Anxiety in Institutions*. London: Free Association Books.

Newham Area Child Protection Committee (2002) *Ainlee*. London Borough of Newham.

Norris, D. (1990) *Violence Against Social Workers: The Implications for Practice*. London: Jessica Kingsley Publishers.

Nursten, J. and Smith, M. (1996) 'Believe or disbelieve? With particular reference to Satanist abuse.' *Child Abuse Review 5*, 4, 253–262.

Obholzer, A. and Roberts, V. (1994) *The Unconscious at Work: Individual and Organisational Stress in the Human Services*. London: Routledge.

Ofshe, R. and Watters, E. (1995) *Making Monsters: False Memories, Psychotherapy and Sexual Hysteria*. London: Andre Deutsch.

Parkinson, F. (1993) *Post-trauma Stress*. London: Sheldon Press.

Phillips, A. (1997) *Terrors and Experts*. London: Faber and Faber.

Prins, H. (1988) 'Dangerous clients: further observations on the limitations of mayhem.' *British Journal of Social Work 18*, 6, 593–609.

Punter, D. (1996) *The Literature of Terror. Volume I, The Gothic Tradition*. London: Longman.

Raphael, B. (1990) *When Disaster Strikes – A Handbook for the Caring Professions*. London: Unwin Hyman.

Reith, M. (1998) *Community Care Tragedies: A Practice Guide to Mental Health Inquiries*. Birmingham: Venture Press.

Rigby, J. (2000) *English Gothic: A Century of Horror Cinema*. London: Reynolds and Hearn.

Royle, N. (2003) *The Uncanny*. Manchester University Press.

Ruddock, M. (1998) 'Yes, and but, and then again maybe.' In R. Davies (ed) *Stress in Social Work*. London: Jessica Kingsley Publishers.

Sainsbury Centre (2002) *Breaking the Circles of Fear: A Review of the Relationship between Mental Health Services and African and Caribbean Communities*. London: The Sainsbury Centre.

Sapolsky, R. (1998) *Why Zebras don't get Ulcers: An Updated Guide to Stress, Stress-Related Diseases, and Coping*. New York: W.H. Freeman.

Sargant, W. (1973) *The Mind Possessed: A Psychology of Possession, Mysticism and Faith Healing*. London: Cox and Wyman.

Scott, R. and Stradling, P. (1993) *Counselling for Post-Traumatic Stress Disorder*. London: Sage.

Sedgwick, E. and Frank, A. (1995) *Shame and its Sisters: A Silvan Tomkins Reader*. London: Duke University Press.

Shakespeare, W. [1606] (1965) *Macbeth*. New York: Airmont.

Shakespeare, W. [1604] (1986) *Hamlet*. Harmondsworth: Penguin.

Shakespeare, W. [1603] (1987) *Othello*. Essex: Longman.

Shelley, M. [1818] (1994) *Frankenstein, or, The Modern Prometheus*. Hertfordshire: Wordsworth.

Shelley, P. [1818] (1986) *Selected Poems* (edited by T. Webb). London: Everyman.

Shipton, G. (ed) (1997) *Supervision of Psychotherapy and Counselling: Making a Place to Think*. Buckingham: Open University Press.

Sinason, V. (ed) (1994) *Treating Survivors of Satanist Abuse*. London: Routledge.

Sinason, V. (ed) (2002) *Attachment, Trauma and Multiplicity: Working with Dissociative Identity Disorder*. London: Routledge.

Smith, M. (1999) 'Variations on a scream: a journey through post-traumatic stress disorder.' *Journal of Social Work Practice 13*, 1, 29–37.

Smith, M. (2002) 'Embrace the fear.' *Community Care*. 18–24 April, 38.

Smith, M. and Nursten, J. (1998) 'Social workers' experiences of distress – moving towards change?' *British Journal of Social Work 28*, 351–368.

Spielberg, S. (1998) Interview with Tom Shone. *Sunday Times*. 13 September.

Stanford, P. (1998) *The Devil*. London: Arrow.

Stanley, J. and Goddard, C. (2002) *In the Firing Line: Violence and Power in Child Protection Work*. Chichester: John Wiley.

Stevenson, R. [1886] (1974) *The Strange Case of Dr Jekyll and Mr Hyde*. London: New English Library.

Stewart, I. and Joines, V. (2002) *TA Today: A New Introduction to Transactional Analysis*. Nottingham: Lifespace.

Stoker, B. [1897] (1996) *Dracula*. London: Everyman.

Storr, A. (1992) *The Art of Psychotherapy (Second Edition)*. Oxford: Butterworth-Heinemann.

Sullivan, E. (2000) 'Gallows humour in social work practice: an issue for supervision and reflexivity.' *Practice 12*, 2, 311–322.

Tatar, M. (ed) (2003) *The Annotated Classic Fairy Tales*. London: W.W. Norton.

Thompson, R. (1995) *Managing People*. Oxford: Butterworth-Heinemann.

Townsend, D. (1998) 'Stress at the top.' In R. Davies (ed) *Stress in Social Work*. London: Jessica Kingsley Publishers.

Van Heeswyk, P. (1998) 'In the place of the parents: stress in residential social work with children and adolescents.' In R. Davies (ed) *Stress in Social Work*. London: Jessica Kingsley Publishers.

Walsh, J. (2003) *Are You Talking to Me? A Life Through the Movies*. London: HarperCollins.

Ward, A. and McMahon, L. (ed) (1998) *Intuition is not Enough: Matching Learning with Practice in Therapeutic Child Care*. London: Routledge.

Ward, I. (1996) 'Adolescent fantasies and the horror film.' *British Journal of Psychotherapy 13*, 2, 267–276.

Warner, M. (2000) *No Go the Bogeyman: Scaring, Lulling and Making Mock*. London: Vintage.

Webb, L. and McCaffrey, T. (1998) 'Emotional repair for organisations: intervening in the aftermath of trauma.' In R. Davies (ed) *Stress in Social Work*. London: Jessica Kingsley Publishers.

Westheimer, I. (1977) *The Process of Supervision in Social Work*. London: Ward Lock Educational.

Wilde, O. [1896] (1997) *The Ballad of Reading Gaol.* In *The Collected Works of Oscar Wilde.* Hertfordshire: Wordsworth.

Williams, T. (1996) *Hearths of Darkness: The Family in the American Horror Film.* London: Madison N.J.

Winnicott, D.W. (1987) 'Hate in the countertransference.' In *Through Paediatrics to Psychoanalysis: Collected Papers.* London: Karnac.

Wittgenstein, L. (1961) *Tractatus Logico-Philosophicus.* London: Routledge.

Wordsworth, W. [1805] (1970) *The Prelude.* Oxford: Oxford University Press.

Zweig, C. and Abrams, J. (1991) *Meeting the Shadow: The Hidden Power of the Dark Side of Human Nature.* New York: Jeremy Tarcher.

Subject Index

acting out 97
actual bodily harm 92
'adapted child' role 136–7
administrative staff 74–5, 78, 85
affirmation 122–3
African Caribbeans 148
alcohol abuse 28, 54, 56, 59, 63–4, 71,
    77–82, 92, 139
ambivalent attitudes to fear 11, 13–15, 20,
    27–8, 32, 35–6, 43–9, 81, 85, 134
anger 95, 96–7, 98–9
annihilation, fears of 28, 53, 59–61, 71, 81,
    116
anti-establishment groups 75–6, 85
anxiety 61
    definition 25–6
    and fear 25–6
    management as containers for 101, 105,
        106–8, 110–11, 113
    regarding complaints procedures 106–8
    separation anxiety 60, 61, 81, 90, 102,
        132
archetypes
    of fear 21, 31–2, 33–4, 39–40
    hero 69
    shadow 27, 31, 39–41, 42
arson 61–2
art 31, 32
assault see physical assault; rape; sexual assault
attachment figures 11, 15–16, 28, 54–5, 57,
    60, 64, 90, 136
attraction to fear 35–7
authority figures 79, 137

belonging 116, 129
Blake, William 31, 38
blame 106
blame culture 102
Bosch, Hieronymous 31, 38
buildings, under threat 28, 101, 108–11
bullying, workplace 28, 101, 111–13, 114
bureaucracy 101, 113

Carlile, Kimberley 44–6
catharsis 138–9

child care/protection work 27–8, 43–58, 109
    child deaths 43–9, 57
    fear of losing control 55–7
    fear of physical assault 53–5, 87–8
    fear of threats 49–53
    imaginations running riot 49–53
    removal of children 49, 109
    see also young people
child ego states 136–7
child-like responses to fear 29, 136–7, 144
childhood perceptions of fear 27, 31–42
childhood physical abuse 43–9
childhood sexual abuse 22–3, 24, 47, 93
circles of fear 148
Climbié, Victoria 101, 108, 113
colleagues
    dealing with fear through the support of
        28, 39–41, 115–17
    same level 115–17
    sense of community amongst 116, 129
    unhelpful 117–18
collective mind 80–1
collective unconscious 27, 31, 40–1, 42
Colwell, Maria 43
community, sense of 116, 129
Community Care (magazine) 24
community mental health nurses 79
community nurses 103–4
community workers 28, 73–86
competence, undermining 102
    see also incompetence
complacency, guards against 12
complaints 28
    fear of 101–6, 113
    made by young people 95
    management's response to 105, 106–8
confirmation 115
connection 116
consultants 134–5, 144
containment 101, 105–8, 110–11, 113, 119,
    125, 137–8
control, fear of losing/ loss of 28, 43, 55–7,
    92–3, 96, 104, 111
'controlling parent' role 137
coping with fear see dealing with fear
counselling 142
counsellors 76–7, 78, 125, 132–3
countertransference 93
creative writing 140
criticism 46, 57
culture 27, 31–2

Author Index